MW00900455

Santa Claus's
Christmas Trivia Challenge 2:
More than 250 new questions (and answers)
capturing the spirit of Christmas!

Jonathan Ozanne

Copyright © 2014 Jonathan Ozanne

All rights reserved.

ISBN-13: 978-1499343540

ISBN-10: 149934354X

DEDICATION

For Sarah, Josiah, Gideon, and Samuel.

In memory of Micah.

CONTENTS

ACKNOWLEDGMENTS

The author is grateful for the encouragement he has received from his family and friends while writing this book.

Cover Image Credit: Hasloo Studio Group/Shutterstock

INTRODUCTION

I wrote this book because I like celebrating Christmas and I like reading and writing about Christmas. Last year I wrote *Santa Claus's Christmas Trivia Challenge*. There is so much information about Christmas that clearly there was room to write another trivia book, and make that book even better than *Santa Claus's Christmas Trivia Challenge*. To this end, *Santa Claus's Christmas Trivia Challenge 2* features more than 250 new trivia questions about Christmas. The questions cover many new topics and go into greater depth on old topics. You do not need to have read *Santa Claus's Christmas Trivia Challenge* to enjoy this book.

Santa Claus's Christmas Trivia Challenge 2 is fun as an individual or group challenge. The group can play competitively or cooperatively. To keep score it is recommended that the players write their answers (usually whether they choose answer A, B, or C for a particular question) on a piece of paper. Then when they get to the answer section, scoring the answers is easy. Most answers are given in some detail, and many have extra information in them so generally it will not be necessary flip back to the questions to see what was being asked for a given question in order to understand an answer.

I hope you like this book and that it makes you feel good about Christmas!

Have a Merry Christmas!

Jonathan Ozanne

QUESTIONS START HERE

SECTION 1: SANTA CLAUS

Who better to start this book than Santa Claus himself? This first section features questions about Santa Claus. Santa is one of the most recognizable symbols of Christmas. How much do you know about Santa?

1. If you were going to tell someone what Santa Claus looks like, which description would you choose?
    A. Santa is a rich man with a white beard. He used to be a miser. He has seen the error of his selfish greed and now brings gifts to children.
    B. Santa is a stocky and jolly old elf. He has a white beard. He brings gifts to children.
    C. Santa is a goat with a white beard. He plays tricks on Father Christmas.

2. Why does Santa usually wear red?
    A. For proper flying-sleigh safety, bright-colored clothing is needed
    B. For warmth; red is the warmest color and helps Santa stay warm on long sleigh rides
    C. The first color illustrations of Santa showed him wearing red clothes

3. Santa has a list of who has been naughty and who has been _____?
    A. Sort of good
    B. Not that bad
    C. Nice

4. When does Santa deliver gifts?
    A. The night of December 5
    B. The night of December 24
    C. The night of December 26

5. True or False? Santa often eats tasty snacks of milk and cookies while delivering gifts?

6. What animals does Santa use to pull his sleigh?
    A. Reindeer
    B. Goats
    C. Moose

7. What are the names of Santa's reindeer?
    A. Dasher, Dancer, Prancer, Rixen, Comet, Cupid, Donner, Blitzen, and Rudolph
    B. Dasher, Dancer, Prancer, Vixen, Comet, Cupid, Donder, Blitzen, and Rudolph
    C. Dasher, Dancer, Prancer, Vixen, Comment, Cupid, Donder, Blitzen, and Rudolph

8. It is dark at night; which reindeer lights the way for Santa's sleigh?
    A. Dancer
    B. Prancer
    C. Rudolph

9. How does Santa carry the many packages, gifts, and toys that he is bringing to children?
    A. In his pockets
    B. In a suitcase
    C. In a sack

10. Generally, how does Santa enter a home to deliver presents?
    A. He sneaks in the front door
    B. He pries open a window
    C. He slides down the chimney

11. If a home does not have a chimney, or the chimney is too small, what does Santa do?
    A. He skips that home
    B. He uses the window or the front door
    C. Santa is an elf and can enter the home through any tiny opening

12. True or False? North American Aerospace Defense Command (better known as NORAD) tracks Santa each year?

13. When did Santa make his first personal appearance at a store during the Christmas shopping season?
    A. 1840s
    B. 1890s
    C. 1940s

14. When did the idea of having Santa appear in person catch on and become common during the Christmas shopping season?
    A. 1840s
    B. 1890s
    C. 1940s

SECTION 2: FROM SAINT NICHOLAS TO SANTA CLAUS

This next section is about Saint Nicholas and the history of the Santa Claus legend. How much do you know about Saint Nicholas? Do you know how his legend is connected to Santa Claus's story?

15. Coming a month before Epiphany, what day is Saint Nicholas's Day?
   A. December 6
   B. December 13
   C. December 20

16. What happens on the eve of Saint Nicholas's Day?
   A. Saint Nicholas comes bringing gifts for children, and these gifts are left under a tree
   B. Saint Nicholas comes bringing gifts for children, and these gifts are usually left in shoes which have been carefully set aside
   C. Saint Nicholas comes bringing the Christmas tree

17. In Europe, how long has Saint Nicholas's Day been widely observed as a holiday?
   A. Since around 1100 A.D.
   B. Since around 1600 A.D.
   C. Since around 2000 A.D.

18. True or False? Saint Nicholas is a patron saint of both Russia and Greece?

19. Also a symbol for pawnbrokers, which of the following is a symbol of Saint Nicholas?
   A. Three stockings
   B. Three golden balls
   C. Three fish

20. How much do historians know for certain about Saint Nicholas?
   A. They do not know very much for certain about him
   B. They know a lot about him except his childhood and teenage years
   C. Thanks to early biographers, historians have an almost complete picture of the life of Saint Nicholas

21. Appointed bishop nearly 200 years before the fall of Rome, when was Saint Nicholas the Bishop of Myra?
   A. 300s A.D.
   B. 600s A.D.
   C. 900s A.D.

22. Saint Nicholas is known for performing many miracles. At least how many miracles are associated with Saint Nicholas?
    A. 11
    B. 17
    C. 21

23. Saint Nicholas is the Patron Saint of Travelers. He is also known for looking after who?
    A. Children and the poor
    B. Leatherworkers
    C. Weavers

24. Where is Saint Nicholas buried?
    A. Bari, in a special church
    B. Myra, in his hometown
    C. Vatican City, in the Crypt of the Saints

25. In many countries, when Saint Nicholas visits, he is accompanied by a scary assistant who threatens to deal out punishment to bad children. What best describes the figure known as *Zwarte Piet*, (Black Peter) who accompanies Saint Nicholas in Holland?
    A. He is a mischievous Moor from Spain
    B. He is a scary monster
    C. He threatens to capture naughty children

26. Dressed in dark clothes and carrying a large sack, what best describes the figure known as *Schmatzli*, who accompanies *Samichlaus* in Switzerland?
    A. He is a mischievous Moor from Spain
    B. He is a scary monster
    C. He threatens to capture naughty children

27. What best describes the figure known as *Pelznickel* in Germany?
    A. He threatens to whip bad children
    B. He dresses all in furs
    C. He leaves bundles of twigs for bad children

28. What best describes the figure known as *Knecht Ruprecht,* who accompanies Saint Nicholas in Germany?
   A. He threatens to whip bad children
   B. He dresses all in furs
   C. He leaves bundles of twigs for bad children

29. With a long tongue and red fur, what best describes the figure known as *Krampus,* who accompanies Saint Nicholas in Austria?
   A. He is a mischievous Moor from Spain
   B. He is a scary monster
   C. He threatens to capture naughty children

30. Looking like a Santa Claus dressed in black instead of red, what best describes the figure known as *Père Fouettard,* who accompanies *Père Noël* in France?
   A. He threatens to whip bad children
   B. He dresses all in furs
   C. He leaves bundles of twigs for bad children

31. In Holland, what does *Sinterklaas* (Saint Nicholas) wear when he visits?
   A. He wears a bishop's robe and hat
   B. He wears a red jacket with a belt and cap (like Santa Claus wears)
   C. He wears a plain robe and a crown of holly

32. How does Saint Nicholas travel?
   A. On land he travels by white horse
   B. On land he travels by carriage
   C. On land he travels by reindeer and sleigh

33. Did the Protestant Reformation affect Saint Nicholas's Day celebrations in most Protestant countries?
   A. Yes
   B. No

34. What happened to Saint Nicholas's Day in Britain after the Protestant Reformation?
   A. It was renamed Oliver's Day and celebrations resumed
   B. It largely faded away after the establishment of the Anglican Church and after the Puritans banned Christmas celebrations
   C. It was one of the few Catholic customs to remain despite all the religious turmoil

35. Generally what happened to Saint Nicholas's Day in Lutheran areas of what is now Germany?
    A. It was one of the few Catholic customs to remain despite the religious turmoil
    B. It was one of the few Catholic customs to be outlawed during the religious turmoil
    C. The holiday was taken from Saint Nicholas and moved to December 25 and the gift-bringer was said to be an angelic child

36. In Germany, who is *Kris Kringle* and what does he look like?
    A. He is a replacement for Saint Nicholas; he resembles a young dark-haired Santa in his 40s
    B. He is a replacement for Saint Nicholas; he resembles an angelic child
    C. He is a donut salesmen; he has nothing to do with Christmas

37. Why do most Americans celebrate Santa Claus?
    A. The custom of Santa came to America with Dutch immigrants in the 1600s. The Dutch *Sinterklaas* and American Santa Claus are almost identical.
    B. Santa's story was invented by the Coca-Cola™ company in the 1890s as a means to sell more cold beverages during the winter.
    C. Early 19th century American writers wrote about Santa. Their writings were popular and within a few decades Santa became a national and international figure.

38. This famous poem is known by two names and is the foundation for many details about Santa. It helped launch the American custom of hanging Christmas stockings. What is the other name of "Twas the Night before Christmas"?
    A. "Here Comes Santa Claus"
    B. "A Visit from Saint Nicholas"
    C. "Winter Wonderland"

39. What was the name of the girl who wrote a famous letter to the editor of the New York Sun asking if Santa Claus is real?
    A. Anna
    B. Susie
    C. Virginia

40. Did the editor tell the little girl that Santa is real?
    A. Yes
    B. No

SECTION 3: CHRISTMAS CARDS, STOCKINGS, TREES, AND PRESENTS

This next section is about the history of several parts of the modern Christmas celebration, namely cards, stockings, trees, and presents.

41. The first Christmas cards were invented in Britain early in the reign of Queen Victoria. When were the first Christmas cards sent?
    A. 1840s
    B. 1880s
    C. 1940s

42. The idea soon crossed the Atlantic; when were the first Christmas cards sent in the United States?
    A. 1850s
    B. 1890s
    C. 1950s

43. In a calamity that probably had nothing to do with Woodrow Wilson recently being elected president, what year did the volume of Christmas cards sent through the mail get to be so high that the postal system in the United States almost got overwhelmed?
    A. 1873
    B. 1913
    C. 1953

44. Historically postage stamps exclusively depicted heads-of-state. It took decades before other subject matter was depicted. What decade was the first Christmas-themed postage stamp issued?
    A. 1850s
    B. 1880s
    C. 1930s

45. In what Alpine country was the first Christmas-themed postage stamp issued?
    A. Austria
    B. Great Britain
    C. United States

46. What Saint Nicholas legend is the likely source of inspiration for the practice of hanging Christmas stockings?
    A. Saint Nicholas saved three generals from an unjust punishment
    B. Saint Nicholas provided three dowries by secretly placing money in stockings
    C. Saint Nicholas saved three barrels from a fire, thereby saving a brewer from bankruptcy

47. With the publication of the poem "A Visit from Saint Nicholas", the custom of hanging Christmas stockings for Santa soon became popular in the United States. Did author Clement C. Moore describe an existing custom or invent the new custom of hanging stockings for Santa?
    A. He described an existing custom in the Dutch communities of New York City
    B. He invented a new custom

48. True or False? Since their introduction in the United States, Christmas stockings have not changed much compared to Christmas trees?

49. What type of tree are Christmas trees?
    A. Deciduous (lose their leaves in the fall)
    B. Coniferous (stay green all year)

50. The concept of a Christmas tree first came to America from where?
    A. Germany
    B. France
    C. Britain

51. True or False? Martin Luther is a legendary originator of the idea of Christmas trees?

52. Which of the following saints is a legendary originator of the idea of Christmas trees?
    A. Saint Boniface
    B. Saint Elmo
    C. Saint Stephen

53. Which of the following answers is a plausible explanation for the origin of Christmas trees?
    A. The custom of decorating with Christmas trees arose out of medieval Biblical dramas about Adam and Eve
    B. The custom of decorating with Christmas trees arose out of a Turkish custom that was brought to Europe during the Crusades
    C. The custom of decorating with Christmas trees arose out of the practices of Holy Roman Emperor Frederick XCII

54. What do most Christmas historians conclude about the origins of Christmas trees?
    A. Christmas trees have always been a Christian symbol
    B. Christmas trees are among the many pagan winter symbols that have been Christianized and/or secularized as a part of Christmas
    C. Christmas trees originated as a secular symbol rather than as a pagan one

55. Were the original Christmas trees from the late Middle Ages lighted or unlighted?
    A. Lighted
    B. Unlighted

56. Which answer best describes the history of the size of Christmas trees that people used in their homes?
    A. Originally small trees were used, and gradually larger trees were used
    B. Originally larger trees were used, and gradually smaller trees were used
    C. The size of trees used has been remarkably constant since the 1500s

57. In what decade were parallel strand electric lights first put on Christmas trees? (Parallel strands stay lit even if one bulb goes out)
    A. 1870s
    B. 1910s
    C. 1920s

58. Which answer best describes a Christmas tree from the 1500s?
    A. Common only in what is now Germany
    B. Brilliantly lit with electric lights for the first time
    C. Brilliantly lit with candles for the first time
    D. Rapidly gaining popularity across the United States

59. Which answer best describes a Christmas tree from the 1600s?
    A. Common only in what is now Germany
    B. Brilliantly lit with electric lights for the first time
    C. Brilliantly lit with candles for the first time
    D. Rapidly gaining popularity across the United States

60. Which answer best describes a Christmas tree from the 1850s?
    A. Common only in what is now Germany
    B. Brilliantly lit with electric lights for the first time
    C. Brilliantly lit with candles for the first time
    D. Rapidly gaining popularity across the United States

61. Which answer best describes a Christmas tree from the 1900s?
    A. Common only in what is now Germany
    B. Brilliantly lit with electric lights for the first time
    C. Brilliantly lit with candles for the first time
    D. Rapidly gaining popularity across the United States

62. True or False? The industrial revolution helped create the retail side of Christmas?

63. One classic image of Christmas shopping is the store window display. In what decade did Christmas-oriented store window displays become common in the United States?
    A. 1850s
    B. 1870s
    C. 1890s

64. Originally Christmas presents were not wrapped. Why did people begin wrapping Christmas presents?
    A. The gifts from the Magi were wrapped
    B. To protect them while they wait to be opened
    C. To make them special

65. Originally Christmas presents were not wrapped. In 1917, who invented modern wrapping paper?
    A. Joyce Hall, the founder of Hallmark™
    B. Sam Walton, the founder of Wal-Mart™
    C. Alvah Roebuck, a co-founder of Sears, Roebuck and Co.™

66. At first, folds in the paper, string, and ribbons were used to secure wrapping paper. In what decade was tape for wrapping packages invented?
    A. 1920s
    B. 1930s
    C. 1940s

67. Generally what happened to the size of Christmas presents from 1850 until today?
    A. They started small and got larger
    B. They started large and got smaller
    C. They have been the same size

68. What characterized Christmas presents prior to the 1890s?
    A. The gifts were practical gadgets
    B. The gifts were expensive treasures
    C. The gifts were insignificant curios

69. What also characterized Christmas gifts prior to the 1890s?
    A. Very few of the gifts were edible
    B. Many of the gifts were edible

70. A classic Christmas present is a model train. In what decade was the first electric toy train sold?
    A. 1870s
    B. 1900s
    C. 1930s

SECTION 4: CHRISTMAS FOODS

How much do you know about the various special foods and beverages that are consumed during the Christmas season? The questions here cover some foods that you have probably heard of before, and likely a few new ones as well. Lots of good food is eaten during the Christmas season and in terms of the number of questions, this section is barely an appetizer. It would be easy to fill a whole trivia book with nothing but Christmas food and beverage questions.

71. A creamy beverage made with eggs, what is the primary spice in eggnog?
    A. Ginger
    B. Nutmeg
    C. Saffron

72. Gingerbread can be baked hard and then crafted into wonderful candy-coated miniature houses. Where did gingerbread houses originate?
    A. Germany
    B. United Kingdom
    C. United States

73. Since when have ginger-flavored cookies and treats been popular at Christmastime in Europe?
    A. The Middle Ages
    B. Since Victorian times
    C. After World War II

74. True or False? Plums are usually an ingredient in plum pudding?

75. Wassail is a warm beverage that wards off the winter chill and can be made with or without alcohol. (Recipes with alcohol are more common). Which of the following items used to be an ingredient in wassail, but is no longer included in most recipes?
    A. Spiced ale
    B. Buttered toast
    C. Apples

76. A popular food in France, what is *Buche de Noël*?
    A. A sponge cake shaped like a Yule Log
    B. A roast boar ready to serve with an apple
    C. A candy Christmas pyramid representing the Trinity

77. Which of the following foods is a traditional Christmas food in France?
    A. Eels
    B. Oysters
    C. Squid

78. Traditionally, when is the main Christmas dinner, known as *Le Reveillon de Noël*, eaten in France?
    A. After midnight Mass on Christmas Eve
    B. After morning Mass on Christmas Day
    C. Anytime on Christmas Day

79. True or False? *Foie gras* (goose liver) is a traditional Christmas gift in France?

80. What is a *Galette des Rois*?
    A. Saint Nicholas cake
    B. Christmas cake
    C. Epiphany cake

81. Which of the following foods is a traditional Christmas food in Italy?
    A. Eels
    B. Oysters
    C. Squid

82. True or False? Pasta is eaten as part of the Christmas dinner in Italy?

83. Which of the following desserts is a traditional Christmas dessert in Italy?
    A. Apple pie
    B. Fruitcake
    C. Neapolitan ice cream

84. Eaten in Holland, what are *letterbankets*?
    A. Roast ham mini-casseroles
    B. Initial-shaped pastries
    C. Stewed assortment of vegetables

85. What spice is the primary spice in Swedish baked goods that celebrate Saint Lucia Day (December 13)?

    A. Cinnamon

    B. Nutmeg

    C. Saffron

86. An old Norse favorite, what meat is traditionally eaten on Christmas in Sweden?

    A. Lamb

    B. Ham

    C. Beef

87. Which answer best describes a food from Germany called *stollen*?

    A. Fish baked with lye

    B. Fruit bread shaped like a crib

    C. Star shaped fruit slices that are put in punch

88. What is the traditional dessert at a Polish *Wigilia*?

    A. Cinnamon ice cream

    B. Poppy-seed cake

    C. Potato pie

89. Popular in Russia, what is *babka*?

    A. Ice cream

    B. Coffee cake

    C. Cabbage pudding

90. Popular in Quebec, this food is a traditional part of the feast eaten after the Midnight Mass on Christmas Eve; what is *tourtière*?

    A. Pork pie

    B. Beef and dumplings

    C. Chicken casserole

91. At the conclusion of a Christmas meal, where would you be most likely to be served a cake known as *flan* (also popular in Spain)?

    A. Belgium

    B. Philippines

    C. Romania

92. During Advent, where would you be most likely to be served a pastry called *buñuelo*?
    A. Greece
    B. Mexico
    C. Poland

93. On Christmas Eve where would you be most likely to be served a bread known as *oplatek*?
    A. Austria
    B. France
    C. Poland

94. As part of Christmas dinner, where would you most likely to be served a rice pudding where it is customary for everyone to say a rhyme before eating his or her first bite?
    A. Belgium
    B. China
    C. Sweden

SECTION 5: CHRISTMAS AROUND THE WORLD

How much do you know about how Christmas is celebrated in lands both near and far from the United States?

95. True or False? Santa Claus is a common part of Christmas celebrations in Canada?

96. What city in Canada features a rather unique celebration that includes a flotilla of ships and choir concerts during the two weeks prior to Christmas?
      A. Edmonton
      B. Ottawa
      C. Vancouver

97. Nova Scotia, Canada features *belsnicklers* during the 12 Days of Christmas. What are *belsnicklers*?
      A. Costumed people who are rowdy mischief-makers. They both seek and distribute treats.
      B. People who go about the neighborhood laughing in merry fashion
      C. Costumed people who perform outdoor plays based on the Nativity

98. Who brings Christmas presents to British children?
      A. Father Christmas
      B. The Good Goblin
      C. The Three Wise Men

99. Which answer provides the best summary of the description of Father Christmas?
      A. He is the British version of Saint Nicholas
      B. He is a combination of Celtic, Norse, and Victorian influences
      C. He is the British version of Frosty the Snowman

100. One popular tradition in the British Isles are Christmas crackers. Christmas crackers are not food. These tiny noise-makers are wrapped in decorative paper and make a loud pop when they are pulled open. Inside of the wrapper is candy, or piece of paper with a joke written on it, or another small prize. When were Christmas crackers invented?
      A. 1840s
      B. 1860s
      C. 1880s

101. What day is Boxing Day?
    A. December 24
    B. December 25
    C. December 26

102. What happens on Boxing Day?
    A. The heavyweight prize-fighting match
    B. Everyone puts old clothes in boxes
    C. Churches give money to the poor, and workers can collect money from their employers

103. True or False? Piggy banks originated from Boxing Day?

104. Who brings Christmas presents to French children?
    A. Father Christmas
    B. Père Noël
    C. Befana

105. Which Christmas decoration is more likely to be a focal point in a French home - a *crèche* (manger display) or a Christmas tree?
    A. *Crèche*
    B. Christmas tree

106. What country popularized setting up miniature winter village displays as a home interior decoration?
    A. France
    B. Germany
    C. Norway

107. Which of the following countries is most famous for month-long Christmas markets that feature many Christmas-oriented decorations and other goods?
    A. Brazil
    B. Germany
    C. Portugal

108. What best describes a *Julenisse* from Norway?

    A. He is a Christmas Elf

    B. He is a Christmas Troll

    C. He is always helpful

109. True or False? Many children in Italy receive presents on both December 25 and January 6?

110. On what day are Christmas gifts exchanged in Greece?

    A. December 25

    B. January 1

    C. January 6

111. On what day does the Christmas season end in Sweden?

    A. December 26

    B. January 6

    C. January 13

112. What is a common secular activity that takes place in many South American countries on Christmas Day?

    A. Shopping for presents

    B. Sleigh rides

    C. Sporting events

113. On what day do children receive Christmas presents in Chile?

    A. December 6

    B. December 25

    C. January 6

114. On what day do children receive Christmas presents in Colombia?

    A. December 6

    B. December 25

    C. January 6

115. Children from Guatemala find gifts in their shoes on what day?

    A. December 6

    B. December 21

    C. January 6

116. What is the Christmas greeting in Guatemala?
  A. *Feliz Cumpleaños*
  B. *Feliz Navidad*
  C. *Buon Noël*

117. Poinsettias are from what country?
  A. Guatemala
  B. Mexico
  C. Panama

118. What are Mexican *posadas*?
  A. Festivals celebrating the Three Kings
  B. Nightly processions about the Holy Family seeking shelter
  C. Life-size Nativity displays

119. What festival happens in Oaxaca, Mexico on December 23?
  A. Night of the Inn
  B. Night of the Radishes
  C. Night of the Wise Men

120. When do Mexican children receive Christmas presents?
  A. December 6
  B. December 25
  C. January 6

121. On what day does the Christmas season end in Mexico?
  A. January 6
  B. January 27
  C. February 2

122. What country celebrates the baptism of Christ with a three-day holiday called *Timkat* that starts on January 19th?
  A. Austria
  B. Ethiopia
  C. Thailand

123. What is different about how the Western Churches (Roman Catholics and Protestants) celebrate Epiphany versus how the Eastern Churches (Eastern Orthodox Churches, and many Churches in the Middle East and North Africa such as the Coptic Church) celebrate Epiphany?
    A. The two Churches are on different calendars (Gregorian and Julian), and celebrate different events in the life of Jesus on Epiphany
    B. The two Churches are on the same calendar (Gregorian) and celebrate different events in the life of Jesus on Epiphany
    C. There is no difference in the Epiphany celebrations of the Western and Eastern Churches

124. On what day on the Gregorian Calendar do Christians in Egypt celebrate Christmas?
    A. December 24
    B. December 25
    C. January 7

125. Which animal is said to deliver Christmas gifts to children in Lebanon?
    A. Camel
    B. Donkey
    C. Elephant

126. Which of the following is a Christmas decoration in Lebanon?
    A. Christmas pyramids
    B. Christmas sprouting seeds
    C. Christmas fountains

127. Star lanterns called *parols* are a featured Christmas decoration of which nation?
    A. Japan
    B. Philippines
    C. South Korea

128. What country features Christmas Day church services with Nativity plays called *Pastores*?
    A. Japan
    B. Philippines
    C. South Korea

129. What country features a Christmas celebration similar to that of the United States, but the celebration in most of the country is entirely secular?
    A. Japan
    B. Philippines
    C. South Korea

130. What country features early morning Christmas caroling on Christmas Day?
    A. Japan
    B. Philippines
    C. South Korea

131. China has a relatively small number of Christians compared to its total population. Many Chinese who are not Christian celebrate the secular parts of Christmas. Santa Claus is known in China as *Sheng Dan Lao Ren*. What does that name translate to in English?
    A. Father Christmas
    B. Saint Nicholas
    C. Christmas Old Man

132. Christmas celebrations in what country feature summertime community candlelight caroling in city parks?
    A. Australia
    B. China
    C. Vietnam

133. What beverage do children in Australia leave out for Santa at Christmas?
    A. Tea
    B. Cocoa
    C. Lemonade

SECTION 6: CHRISTMAS DECORATIONS AND SYMBOLS

Generally from late November to Christmastime, many streets, yards, homes, churches, schools, and businesses are decorated with symbols of Christmas. Do you know what those symbols are and what those symbols mean?

134. What colors are Christmas colors?
   A. Red and green
   B. Blue and yellow
   C. Purple and orange

135. True or False? Many Christmas symbols and decorations include depictions of the animals, objects, and characters from the Biblical story of Jesus's birth?

136. True or False? Many Christmas symbols and decorations include depictions of objects like bells or candles, that are part of celebrating Christmas?

137. How many candles are in an Advent Wreath?
   A. Advent wreaths never have candles
   B. Three candles
   C. Four candles

138. What do candy canes symbolize?
   A. The North Pole
   B. J for Joseph
   C. A shepherd's crook

139. Which of the following is NOT a Christmas symbol?
   A. Angel
   B. Crown of Thorns
   C. Wreath

140. What do red glass ball ornaments symbolize?
   A. Apples
   B. Sacrifice
   C. Joy

141. When were decorations with small figurines that could depict various scenes from the Nativity developed?
    A. 1200s
    B. 1500s
    C. 1800s

142. How long were the original Yule logs supposed to burn?
    A. 1 night
    B. 7 nights
    C. 12 nights

143. What does the use of light as a decoration at Christmas symbolize?
    A. The Sun
    B. Christ as Light of the World
    C. The Christmas Star

144. In most American towns in December at night, the town will be lit up with outdoor Christmas lights and feature various Christmas-themed displays on front lawns. When did decorating with outdoor electric Christmas lights become common?
    A. 1920s
    B. 1950s
    C. 1980s

145. Originally a pagan symbol, what does mistletoe symbolize in a Christian context?
    A. Christ is Love
    B. Christ the Healer
    C. Christ the King of kings

146. Originally a pagan symbol, what does holly symbolize in a Christian context?
    A. Joy
    B. Peace
    C. Strength

147. What else does holly symbolize in a Christian context?
    A. Gluttony
    B. Suffering
    C. Ash Wednesday

148. Originally a pagan symbol, what does ivy symbolize in a Christian context?

  A. Human weakness and divine strength

  B. Kindness

  C. Mercy

149. Originally a pagan symbol, what does bay (laurel) symbolize in a Christian context?

  A. Christ's victory over sin and death

  B. Christ's victory over the Pharisees

  C. Christ's victory over evil

150. When did cradles become a symbol of Christmas?

  A. Shortly after Christmas became a Christian holiday

  B. In the Middle Ages

  C. In Victorian times

SECTION 7: CHRISTMAS MUSIC

The focus of this section is on religious Christmas carols. Around half of the questions are about the lyrics of carols. If you are familiar with the carol the answer should be fairly clear after a moment of thought. The other half of the section has more obscure questions about history of some of the carols. Generally these history questions will be challenging even if you know the lyrics of the particular carol in question.

151. Carols are sacred folk music used to teach Bible lessons, although the term carol is sometimes used to refer to Christmas music regardless of whether the music is secular or sacred. When are the earliest Christmas carols from?
    A. 900s
    B. 1200s
    C. 1500s

152. Based on the lyrics, which carol depicts a calm and peaceful setting for the Nativity?
    A. "Angels We Have Heard on High"
    B. "I Saw Three Ships"
    C. "Silent Night"

153. Count carefully; in the carol "The Twelve Days of Christmas", how many birds are in the song?
    A. Six
    B. Ten
    C. Twenty-three

154. What time of day does "Jingle Bells" take place?
    A. Morning
    B. Noon
    C. Night

155. There are many carols that tell all or part of the Nativity story. Some carols focus on particular characters from the story. Who is "Angels from the Realms of Glory" about?
    A. Angels
    B. Magi
    C. Shepherds
    D. All three (Angels, Magi, and Shepherds)

156. There are many carols that tell all or part of the Nativity story. Some carols focus on particular characters from the story. Who is "As with Gladness" about?

    A. Angels

    B. Magi

    C. Shepherds

    D. All three (Angels, Magi, and Shepherds)

157. There are many carols that tell all or part of the Nativity story. Some carols focus on particular characters from the story. Who is "Go Tell It on the Mountain" about?

    A. Angels

    B. Magi

    C. Shepherds

    D. All three (Angels, Magi, and Shepherds)

158. There are many carols that tell all or part of the Nativity story. Some carols focus on particular characters from the story. Who is "The First Noel" about?

    A. Angels

    B. Magi

    C. Shepherds

    D. All three (Angels, Magi, and Shepherds)

159. Which of the following phrases is the ending of the last line of the third verse of "Silent Night"?

    A. "Sleep in heavenly peace"

    B. "Christ the Savior is born"

    C. "Jesus, Lord at thy birth"

160. True or False? The fifth verse of "Thou Didst Leave Thy Throne" refers to the Second Coming?

161. What word ends all four verses of "There's a Song in the Air"?

    A. Bring

    B. King

    C. Lord

162. Finish the line from "O Come All Ye Faithful". "Born the King of _____"?
    A. Angels
    B. Humanity
    C. Israel

163. What do the angels have in "It Came upon a Midnight Clear"?
    A. Cymbals of gold
    B. Harps of gold
    C. Trumpets of gold

164. What is the Child doing in "What Child Is This"?
    A. Blessing the animals
    B. Sleeping on Mary's lap
    C. The song does not say

165. What do the angels sing in "Hark the Herald Angels Sing"?
    A. "Glory to the newborn King"
    B. "Let the Heavens ring"
    C. "Praises to our glorious King"

166. What are the cattle doing in "Away in a Manger"?
    A. "Bleating"
    B. "Lowing"
    C. "Mooing"

167. Which of the following carols does not mention myrrh?
    A. "Joy to the World"
    B. "We Three Kings"
    C. "What Child Is This"

168. Which of the following carols urges hearers to come to Bethlehem?
    A. "Angels We Have Heard on High"
    B. "The First Noel"
    C. "O Little Town of Bethlehem"

169. Where did "Jingle Bells" originate?

     A. It was first sung at an Albany sleigh party

     B. It was first sung at a Boston Sunday School

     C. It was first sung at a church in Charleston

170. The song "Santa Claus Is Coming to Town" was written to bring hope in the Great Depression. When was that song written?

     A. 1930s

     B. 1940s

     C. 1950s

171. A famous African-American carol, when was the spiritual "Go Tell It on the Mountain" first published?

     A. 1700s

     B. 1800s

     C. 1900s

172. Which of the following songs is also a spiritual?

     A. "The First Noel"

     B. "Rise Up Shepherds and Follow"

     C. "Here We Come a Wassailing"

173. Which carol is based on Job 38:7?

     A. "God Rest Ye Merry Gentlemen"

     B. "Angels from the Realms of Glory"

     C. "The Friendly Beasts"

174. Which carol had the original Latin title "In Sweet Shouting"?

     A. "Good Christian Men Rejoice"

     B. "O Holy Night"

     C. "Blessed Assurance"

175. How many verses did the original version of "Luther's Cradle Hymn" (now known as "Away in a Manger") have?

     A. One

     B. Two

     C. Three

176. Which carol did Henry Longfellow write?
    A. "I Heard the Bells on Christmas"
    B. "It Came upon a Midnight Clear"
    C. "Good King Wenceslaus"

177. Trailing only its Austrian cousin, which carol is generally acclaimed to be the second most widely-translated carol?
    A. "O Come All Ye Faithful"
    B. "Silent Night"
    C. "Jingle Bells"

178. Which carol was inspired by a pilgrimage to Bethlehem?
    A. "O Little Town of Bethlehem"
    B. "Angels and the Shepherds"
    C. "In the Bleak Midwinter"

179. Which carol has music from Handel's *Messiah*?
    A. "Angels We Have Heard on High"
    B. "Coventry Carol"
    C. "Joy to the World"

180. Which of the following carols comes from a medieval liturgy?
    A. "O Come All Ye Faithful"
    B. "O Come O Come Emmanuel"
    C. "Lo How a Rose E'er Blooming"

181. Which carol was performed for the first time on Christmas Eve in 1847?
    A. "Silent Night"
    B. "Carol of the Bells"
    C. "O Holy Night"

182. Who wrote the music to "Silent Night"?
    A. Franz Grüber
    B. Felix Mendelssohn
    C. Johann Strauss, Sr.

183. William Dix wrote the words to "What Child Is This" and "As with Gladness"; what was his day job?

    A. Church organist

    B. Insurance salesman

    C. Physician

184. What language was the first carol written in North America sung in?

    A. French

    B. Spanish

    C. Huron

185. Which carol was written by a woman, Cecil Frances Alexander, who was a pioneer of the idea of Sunday School?

    A. "Once in Royal David's City"

    B. "Thou Didst Leave Thy Throne"

    C. "The First Noel"

186. Which carol was traditionally sung outdoors at Yule log ceremonies?

    A. "The First Noel"

    B. "In the Bleak Midwinter"

    C. "Away in a Manger"

187. Who wrote a poem called "A Christmas Carol" that later became the carol "In the Bleak Midwinter"?

    A. Christina Rossetti

    B. Katherine Lee Bates

    C. Valerie Starocz

188. What is the origin of the talking beasts speaking in the carol "The Friendly Beasts"?

    A. The imagination of the composer

    B. The Bible

    C. Legends that the animals can talk at midnight on Christmas

189. Which carol is based on 2 Corinthians 5:19?

    A. "Joy to the World"

    B. "Angels We Have Heard on High"

    C. "Hark the Herald Angels Sing"

SECTION 8: CHRISTMAS IN BOOKS AND MOVIES

This section has questions about a small sampling of Christmas-themed books and movies. Although most of the questions ask for main points rather than obscure details about a particular work, it will obviously help immensely if you have read or seen the work in question. Of the stories and movies covered here, maybe you will find a new one to try this year. Of course many of the works listed here are classics and worth being read or watched each year.

190. True or False? *Little Women* by Louisa May Alcott has the message that love and family are more important than fancy gifts at Christmas?

191. Edmund Gwenn portrayed Santa in *Miracle on 34th Street* (1947), and so far is the only actor to receive an Oscar for playing Santa. His portrayal was very convincing. Were his weight and beard real or were they achieved with make-up and special effects?
    A. His beard and weight were real
    B. His beard and weight were achieved with make-up and special effects

192. In the Christmas-themed Sherlock Holmes mystery "The Adventure of the Blue Carbuncle", what role does the goose play in the story?
    A. Holmes and Watson are eating Christmas goose when the mystery commences
    B. A Christmas goose is involved in a case of mistaken identity
    C. A Christmas goose is stolen and Holmes recovers it

193. "Papa Panov: A Christmas Musical" is based on a short story by Leo Tolstoy. It tells the story of an old man trying to live life according to the Gospels. What is the message of "Papa Panov"?
    A. Follow the Ten Commandments
    B. Heal the sick even if they are social outcasts
    C. Treat everyone like you would treat Jesus

194. Ghosts are normally associated with Halloween. How many spirits appear in Charles Dickens's *A Christmas Carol*?
    A. One
    B. Three
    C. Four

195. This character's name is now a synonym for "greedy miser". What is the name of the greedy miser in Charles Dickens's *A Christmas Carol*?
    A. Fezziwig
    B. Scrooge
    C. Tiny Tim

196. What Christmas movie features a future governor of California and the crazed search for a popular toy?
  A. *Home Alone*
  B. *Jingle All the Way*
  C. *Toy Story*

197. What potentially dangerous toy does Ralphie want in the movie *A Christmas Story*?
  A. BB gun
  B. Bike
  C. Nintendo

198. True or False? Actress Julia Dreyfus appears in *Christmas Vacation*?

199. What is the name of the children's story where a boy takes a train to the North Pole?
  A. *North to Alaska*
  B. *Polar Express*
  C. *Santa's Railway*

200. Who does the Grinch dress up as a reindeer in the story *How the Grinch Stole Christmas*?
  A. His dog
  B. Horton
  C. Yertle

201. In the O. Henry short story "The Gift of the Magi" what does the man sell?
  A. He sells his car
  B. He sells his telescope
  C. He sells his watch

202. Which of the following other holidays did author Louisa May Alcott, originator of Santa's Elves, write about?
  A. Father's Day
  B. Labor Day
  C. Thanksgiving

203. What did author Katherine Lee Bates contribute to the Santa Claus story?
  A. Leaving food out for Santa
  B. Mrs. Claus
  C. Both A and B

204. In *A Charlie Brown Christmas*, what type of Christmas tree does Charlie Brown buy?
    A. A large artificial tree
    B. A small artificial tree
    C. A small real tree

205. Which Christmas movie features a taxi driver and a policeman named Bert and Ernie?
    A. *It's a Wonderful Life*
    B. *Miracle on 34th Street*
    C. *White Christmas*

206. What is the message of the Pearl S. Buck short story "Christmas Day in the Morning"?
    A. Be sure to tell a loved one that you love him or her
    B. Do not forget to milk the cows
    C. The best presents come from the heart

207. In *Ramona and Her Father* by Beverly Cleary, Ramona is a sheep in the Christmas pageant. What role does Ramona's sibling, Beezus, play?
    A. Mary
    B. Joseph
    C. Gabriel

208. Although not a Christmas story, *The Wind and the Willows* does have a few winter scenes, including one during the Christmas season. Rat and Mole are visited by some carolers. Which answer best describes the phrase at the end of each verse of the carol?
    A. Alleluia tonight
    B. Rejoice now
    C. Joy in the morning

209. What are the oxen doing in the poem "The Oxen" by Thomas Hardy?
    A. Kneeling
    B. Praying
    C. Singing

210. True or False? G.K. Chesterton wrote a poem about the Nativity and the name of the poem was "A Christmas Carol"?

211. What best describes the feelings of the narrator of Robert Louis Stevenson's poem "Christmas at Sea"?
    A. Happiness at being on vacation
    B. Sadness that turns to happiness
    C. Regret at being away from family at Christmas

212. At Christmas in *Little House in the Big Woods,* what is Laura concerned about?
    A. That her cousins will arrive safely from Tennessee
    B. That she gets enough presents
    C. That Santa will not come unless she falls asleep

213. In *Little House on the Prairie,* does Laura receive more edible or more inedible items in her Christmas stocking?
    A. She receives more edible items
    B. She receives more inedible items
    C. She receives the same number of each

214. In *The Lion, the Witch, and the Wardrobe* by C.S. Lewis, who keeps Father Christmas away until Aslan intervenes?
    A. Puddleglum
    B. White Witch
    C. Black Dwarf

SECTION 9: CHRISTMAS IN THE BIBLE

As a religious holiday, Christmas celebrates the birth of Jesus. That story is told in the Bible. How well do you know the story of Jesus's birth?

215. Who decreed a census that was in effect when Jesus was born?
   A. Caesar Augustus
   B. Julius Caesar
   C. Quirinius

216. What city was Jesus born in?
   A. Bethlehem
   B. Jerusalem
   C. Nazareth

217. Where was Jesus born?
   A. In the inn
   B. In the stable
   C. In the palace

218. What type of structure was the stable?
   A. Wooden barn
   B. Mud hut
   C. Small cave

219. Jesus's birth was first announced to whom?
   A. Shepherds
   B. Wise Men
   C. King Herod

220. In what direction did the Wise Men see a star?
   A. North
   B. South
   C. East

221. Are there independent records of significant astronomical observances that reasonably could be the star mentioned in the Bible?
   A. Yes
   B. No

222. What gifts do the Wise Men bring to Jesus?

    A. Gold, Aloe, Myrrh

    B. Gold, Aloe, Frankincense

    C. Gold, Frankincense, Myrrh

223. How many Wise Men are mentioned in the Bible?

    A. 3

    B. 4

    C. No exact number is given

224. In the Gospel of Saint Matthew, the genealogy of Jesus is traced back to whom?

    A. Abraham

    B. Adam

    C. God

225. In the Gospel of Saint Luke, the genealogy of Jesus is traced back to whom?

    A. Abraham

    B. Adam

    C. God

226. Who was the mother of John the Baptist?

    A. Mary

    B. Elizabeth

    C. Hannah

227. Who was the father of John the Baptist?

    A. Ezra

    B. Isaiah

    C. Zechariah

228. What is the name of the angel who appears to Mary?

    A. Gabriel

    B. Matthew

    C. Michael

229. "Suddenly a multitude of the heavenly host appeared"…what is a heavenly host?
    A. Angelic servants
    B. Angelic choir
    C. Angelic army

230. Which gospel mentions the donkey and the oxen?
    A. Saint Matthew
    B. Saint Luke
    C. Neither

231. Which gospel has Jesus presented at the Temple?
    A. Saint Matthew
    B. Saint Luke
    C. Both

232. Who blessed Jesus at the Temple?
    A. Caiaphas
    B. Simeon
    C. Zechariah

233. Which gospel has the story of the Magi?
    A. Saint Matthew
    B. Saint Luke
    C. Both

234. Which gospel has the story of the flight to Egypt?
    A. Saint Matthew
    B. Saint Luke
    C. Neither

235. After Jesus's birth, what is the next episode that is recorded by all four gospels?
    A. Jesus's ministry as a boy
    B. Jesus selects his disciples
    C. Jesus is baptized by John the Baptist

236. Which book of the Bible identifies Jesus as the "Prince of Peace"?
    A. Isaiah
    B. Micah
    C. Gospel of Saint John

237. Which book of the Bible foretells where Jesus will be born?
    A. Isaiah
    B. Micah
    C. Gospel of Saint John

238. Which book of the Bible identifies Jesus as "Wonderful Counselor"?
    A. Isaiah
    B. Micah
    C. Gospel of Saint John

239. Which book of the Bible identifies Jesus as the "Light of the World"?
    A. Isaiah
    B. Micah
    C. Gospel of Saint John

240. What does the word Christ mean?
    A. Savior
    B. King
    C. Son

SECTION 10: CHRISTMAS CELEBRATION HISTORY

How much do you know about what Christmastime has been like through the ages?

241. True or False? Easter was celebrated as a Christian holiday before Christmas was celebrated as a Christian holiday?

242. Which of the following was NOT a pre-Christian religious festival held within a few weeks of the Winter Solstice?
    A. *Invictus Sol*
    B. *Saturnalia*
    C. *Samhain*

243. What was the name of the holiday from Ancient Rome that included exchanging gifts?
    A. *Kalends*
    B. *Odinday*
    C. *Jul*

244. True or False? Odin from Norse mythology brought gifts in the winter?

245. Which answer best describes a Christmas celebration in the year 100 A.D.?
    A. Feasting, pranks, and merry-making
    B. Solemn religious occasion
    C. Lots of presents
    D. None of the above

246. Which answer best describes a Christmas celebration in Rome in the year 400 A.D.?
    A. Feasting, pranks, and merry-making
    B. Solemn religious occasion
    C. Lots of presents
    D. None of the above

247. What was the first government to recognize Christmas as a legal holiday?
    A. Roman Empire
    B. Byzantine Empire
    C. Viking Empire

248. Which answer best describes a Christmas celebration in England in the year 1400 A.D.?
   A. Feasting, pranks, and merry-making
   B. Solemn religious occasion
   C. Lots of presents
   D. None of the above

249. True or False? In the Middle Ages, Christmastime represented a rare holiday from work during the year?

250. When are the Twelve Days of Christmas?
   A. December 1 through December 12
   B. December 13 through December 25
   C. December 25 through January 6

251. Who is the Lord of Misrule?
   A. A medieval Halloween character who has nothing to do with Christmas
   B. A person who was appointed to cause mischief during the 12 Days of Christmas
   C. A Persian custom that was adapted into Christmas after the Crusades

252. Who are mummers?
   A. Actors from a medieval play
   B. People who throw dried flowers (chrysanthemums) during Epiphany
   C. Fishermen who catch large fish for Christmas dinner

253. What happens to the person who gets the bean in his or her slice of Twelfth Night cake?
   A. That person will have good luck in next year
   B. That person will have bad luck in the next year
   C. That person is made king or queen of the party but must host next year's party

254. Which answer best describes a Christmas celebration in England in the year 1650 A.D.?
   A. Feasting, pranks, and merry-making
   B. Solemn religious occasion
   C. Lots of presents
   D. None of the above

255. Most modern American Christmas customs, such as Santa, Christmas trees, and presents, first came together when?
    A. 1760s
    B. 1860s
    C. 1960s

256. Which president was the first one to have a Christmas tree?
    A. Franklin Pierce
    B. Abraham Lincoln
    C. Ulysses Grant

257. Did the American Civil War and the Reconstruction help or hinder the spread of Christmas as a national holiday?
    A. Helped it
    B. Hindered it
    C. No effect

258. Which holiday became a federal holiday first, Thanksgiving or Christmas?
    A. Thanksgiving
    B. Christmas
    C. They both became holidays at the same time

259. True or False? In the early 1900s, Christmas was also marked by large public feasts for the poor and homeless?

260. If you could time travel, what is approximately the earliest time you could go back to and Christmas morning would most look like how it is observed today in the United States with regards to Christmas trees and presents?
    A. 1950s
    B. 1920s
    C. 1890s

261. If you could time travel and you like Santa Claus, Christmas presents, Christmas trees, Christmas decorations (such as holly and mistletoe), Christmas foods, and many other ideas seemingly adapted from pre-Christian pagans, who should you go back and time and thank?
    A. Pope Leo I
    B. Pope Gregory I
    C. Charlemagne

262. Which answer best describes a Christmas celebration in the United States in the year 2000 A.D.?

   A. Feasting, pranks, and merry-making
   B. Solemn religious occasion
   C. Lots of presents
   D. None of the above

ANSWERS START HERE

<u>SANTA CLAUS</u>

1. B. Santa is best described as a jolly and stocky elf with a white beard who brings gifts to children.

2. C. The first drawings of Santa were black and white sketches. When he first appeared in color artwork, in "Santa Claus and His Works" (1886) by author George P. Webster and illustrator Thomas Nast, red was chosen as the color for his clothes. Red was chosen largely to demonstrate the capabilities of the color printing process. Today, Santa knows that people, particularly children, expect him to wear red, so he obliges them.

3. C. Santa has a list of who has been naughty and who has been nice.

4. B. Santa delivers gifts on the night of December 24th.

5. True. It is traditional to leave a snack for Santa. He gets hungry while delivering gifts.

6. A. Santa's sleigh is pulled by reindeer.

7. B. Santa's reindeer are named: Dasher, Dancer, Prancer, Vixen, Comet, Cupid, Donder (also spelled Donner), Blitzen, and Rudolph.

8. C. Rudolph the red-nosed reindeer lights the way for Santa's sleigh.

9. C. Santa carries the gifts that he is going to deliver in a sack.

10. C. Santa generally uses a chimney to get into a home.

11. C. Santa is a "jolly old elf" and most of the writers who have addressed the issue of how Santa gets into difficult homes have explained that because Santa is an elf he is able to enter a home through any small opening, not just a chimney. A few other writers have said that Santa enlists the aid of others such as parents to deliver presents when Santa is not able to get into the house.

12. True. NORAD has a website that tracks Santa's progress each year. http://www.noradsanta.org

13. A. The first Santa appeared at a store in Philadelphia in 1841 as *Kris Kringle*. Today, in the United States, *Kris Kringle* is a synonym for Santa Claus.

14. B. It was not until the 1890s that the idea of having Santa make personal appearances during the Christmas shopping season caught on and became an annual occurrence. This decade was also when the idea of having Santa Claus endorse products really took off and Santa appeared in advertisements endorsing numerous products.

FROM SAINT NICHOLAS TO SANTA CLAUS

15. A. December 6 is Saint Nicholas's Day. Saint Nicholas died on December 6, 343 A.D. Saint Nicholas's Day is celebrated in many countries, particularly in Europe. A month later on January 6, or Epiphany is the celebration of the arrival of the Wise Men.

16. B. Generally on the night of December 5, Saint Nicholas comes bringing gifts for children. His gifts are usually left in shoes which have been left where Saint Nicholas can find them. Sometimes Saint Nicholas comes to town on December 4, to do some last minute checking on whether children have been good before making his rounds to distribute gifts on the night of December 5.

17. A. In Europe, Saint Nicholas's Day has been widely celebrated since around 1100 A.D., during the Middle Ages. The popularity of Saint Nicholas in western Europe increased after his remains were moved to Bari. The celebration of his holiday sometimes (but not necessarily) coincided with the spread of Christianity into a particular area. Ironically, the people of Bari are proud of having Saint Nicholas buried in their city but he is not part of their Christmas celebrations.

18. True. Saint Nicholas is a patron saint of both Russia and Greece. He is not the only patron saint of either country. Myra, where Saint Nicholas was a bishop, is located in present-day Turkey, but is not that far from Greece. The story of Saint Nicholas spread rapidly with Christianity in Russia in the late 900s, particularly after Prince Vladimir of Kiev married the Princess Anna from the Byzantine Empire.

19. B. Three golden balls representing the three dowries that Saint Nicholas helped a poor family pay so that three daughters could get married. Saint Nicholas is believed to have anonymously placed money in stockings hanging by the fireplace to dry.

20. A. Historians know very little for certain about Saint Nicholas.

21. A. Historians do know that Saint Nicholas was Bishop of Myra in the 300s A.D. Myra is on the southwest coast of present-day Turkey. He is known to have been present at the Council of Nicaea in 325.

22. C. At least 21 miracles are associated with Saint Nicholas. Among the most famous include providing three dowries, saving three generals from an unjust punishment, healing three children, and saving sailors in troubled seas.

23. A. Saint Nicholas is also known for looking after children and the poor. He is the Patron Saint of Children. He has a large saintly portfolio and given this large portfolio has a reputation as a hard-working saint. The legends of Saint Nicholas are full of stories of Saint Nicholas generously helping those in need and those facing injustice.

24. A. Saint Nicholas was originally buried near Myra but in 1087 his remains were moved to Bari, Italy and reburied. The main reason his remains were moved by the citizens of Bari was to create a pilgrimage site in Bari.

25. A. *Zwarte Piet* (Black Peter) is a mischievous Moor from Spain. According to the Dutch, Saint Nicholas spends most of his time in Spain compiling a list of good and bad children. *Zwarte Piet* is mischievous but he also helps Saint Nicholas with gift deliveries.

26. C. *Schwartzi* captures naughty children in a bag. He dresses in dark rags and has a long scruffy beard. He accompanies *Samichlaus* on his visits to deliver gifts to children. *Samichlaus* is the German/Swiss word for Saint Nicholas.

27. B. The sidekick *Pelznickel* from Germany dresses all in furs. His name means furred-Nicholas and has many alternate and regional spellings. *Pelznickel* is often described as also being covered in soot.

28. C. The sidekick *Knecht Ruprecht* from Germany leaves bundles of twigs for bad children. He dresses in rags and threatens to steal or beat bad children. He and *Pelznickel* are regional variations of the same helper.

29. B. *Krampus* is a mischievous monster with red fur, bulging eyes, and a long, red tongue. December 5 is *Krampus* Day in Austria. *Krampus* tries to scare kids into being good.

30. A. *Père Fouettard* threatens to whip bad children. He is a butcher from one of the legends about Saint Nicholas. According to legend, *Père Fouettard* badly mistreated some children and Saint Nicholas restored them to health. In France, *Père Fouettard* also helps *Père Noël* deliver presents as punishment for his past misdeeds.

31. A. In Holland, *Sinterklaas* (Saint Nicholas) wears the vestments of a bishop including a red robe and a mitered hat, and he carries a shepherd's staff. He also carries a book with the names of the good children and bad children.

32. A. On land Saint Nicholas travels by white horse, not by reindeer and sleigh. Interestingly, if stories about Odin from Norse mythology and stories about Saint Nicholas are compared, there are some superficial similarities. For example, they both ride white horses. Likely what happened is that as the story of Saint Nicholas reached Scandinavia and Germany during the Middle Ages, the stories about Odin and stories about Saint Nicholas got mangled together. (During this period of relatively low literacy, most stories were passed on through an oral tradition. Also during this period the people of Scandinavia and Germany were converted to Christianity.) However, there are significant differences between Odin and Saint Nicholas and it would be a mistake to think that the story of Saint Nicholas was stolen from the Norse.

33. A. Yes, the Protestant Reformation had a major impact on how Christmas was celebrated both in terms of in church and in terms of secular traditions. With the Protestant Reformation, the importance of saints was greatly reduced in Protestant communities. Generally this change to Protestantism occurred in northern Europe, parts of Germany, Scandinavia, and parts of the British Isles.

34. B. Saint Nicholas's Day largely faded away in Britain during the 1500s and 1600s. Saint Nicholas was a teenager when he became a bishop. A Saint Nicholas-related custom in Europe that was particularly popular in Britain that was that of the Boy Bishop. A boy would be appointed bishop from December 6 to December 28. Originally the Boy Bishop did a serious job of serving as a priest and in doing so, honoring Saint Nicholas. Later the presence of the Boy Bishop became an excuse for wild behavior from parishioners during church services. The custom of a Boy Bishop was ended during the religious turmoil under the reign of Henry VIII. In 21st century Britain, the Boy Bishop custom has been making a bit of comeback.

35. C. Generally in Lutheran areas of Germany, the holiday was moved to December 25 and the gift-bringer was said to be a Jesus and later said to be an angelic child. The name *Christkind* refers to Jesus as the gift-bringer but the name still applies to the angelic child.

36. B. *Kris Kringle* is another name of the *Christkind* who replaced Saint Nicholas as a gift-bringer in parts of Germany and who made his deliveries on December 25. He

resembles an angelic child. It is said that a bell rings when he has finished his delivery. He enters homes by flying through an open window. Rather confusingly, in the United States, *Kris Kringle* is now a synonym for Santa.

37. C. Early 19th century American writers such as Washington Irving and Clement C. Moore wrote about Santa. The Santa that Moore wrote about was a combination of various Saint Nicholas descriptions from different countries. Moore combined Saint Nicholas and his scary helper into a single figure – Santa Claus. Moore also gave Santa reindeer which vaguely resemble the goats that Odin from Norse mythology had to drive his chariot. Moore did not document his sources of inspiration for Santa Claus. Moore's Santa was also shorter than Santa is shown as today. Moore wrote the Santa Claus story as a private story for his family. As a serious author he wanted to be careful with his reputation. However, the story leaked out and was very popular. About fifteen years after the story was first published, Moore publicly took credit for it. Coca-Cola's™ efforts to advertise with Santa helped polish the modern appearance of Santa that we know today; particularly the work of artist Haddon Sundblom in the 1940s and 50s. However, Coca-Cola™ did not invent Santa.

38. B. "A Visit from Saint Nicholas" by Clement C. Moore is largely responsible for many ideas about Santa such as his appearance, what he does, and how he travels. Artist Thomas Nast discovered that Santa Claus lives at the North Pole. Through his drawings, Thomas Nast did a lot to create the image of Santa that we have today. Nast with his drawings and other writers through various stories have added to Moore's ideas about Santa. Many Santa Claus historians say that the image of Santa Claus was shaped by three people: writer Clement C. Moore, artist Thomas Nast, and artist Haddon Sundblom.

39. C. Virginia wrote a famous letter in 1897 to the New York Sun asking if there was a Santa Claus.

40. A. In short the editor replied, "yes, Virginia there is a Santa Claus". The letter and response were reprinted every year in the New York Sun until 1950 when the Sun went out of business. The letter and response were widely reprinted in other newspapers over the years. With such massive circulation, the letter and response were highly influential in the shaping of opinion about Santa Claus and the use of the Santa Claus legend at Christmas. The response helped make it ok and socially acceptable to believe in Santa. The editor who wrote the response, Francis Church, was never credited with writing it in his lifetime.

CHRISTMAS CARDS, TREES, STOCKINGS, & PRESENTS

41. A. The first Christmas cards were sent in the 1840s in Britain. Sir Henry Cole developed them as a convenience for people who did not have time to write a personal letter at the end of the year to friends and acquaintances. British merchant John Calcott Horsley was the first person to sell them. Christmas cards became much more popular in the later part of the 19th century.

42. A. The first Christmas cards were sent in the United States in the 1850s. The British cards tended to be more luxurious, and the American cards tended to be cheaper than the British ones. Louis Prang was one of the first merchants to sell Christmas cards in the United States. In the United States in the 1950s, families and businesses routinely sent hundreds of cards. That number has moderated somewhat today.

43. B. In January, 1913 the American mail system almost crashed due to the high volume of Christmas cards and packages being sent through it. The volume spiked because the U.S. Postal Service began offering a new delivery service by motorized truck. The postal service was not prepared for the massive demand that this new service created as the system was flooded with new mail that might not have otherwise been sent.

44. C. In 1936, the first Christmas-themed postage stamp was issued. It featured "Madonna and Child" and was based on a painting by Albrecht Dürer. (In December of 1898, Canada issued a stamp about the vast size British Empire. The artwork for the stamp was a map of the world, with a caption about the vast size of the British Empire. The phrase "Xmas 1898" was typewritten on the stamp. Printing that phrase did not make it a Christmas-themed stamp. The theme of the 1898 stamp was the British Empire.)

45. A. The first Christmas-themed stamp was issued in Austria (the stamp described in the previous answer). Great Britain did not issue a Christmas-themed stamp until 1967. The United States did not issue a Christmas-themed stamp until 1962. In the United States, starting in 1907, Christmas seals, which resembled postage stamps, were sold to raise money to fight tuberculosis. These seals were characterized by Christmas-themed artwork and a cross with two crossbars (known as the Cross of Lorraine). Although they resembled stamps, they were not postage stamps and a letter with a Christmas seal still needed a regular stamp to go through the mail.

46. B. Saint Nicholas providing three dowries by placing money in stockings is the likely source of inspiration for the practice of hanging Christmas stockings.

47. B. In "A Visit from Saint Nicholas", Moore invented the custom of hanging stockings for Santa Claus on Christmas Eve. Clement C. Moore's poem "A Visit from Saint Nicholas", also known as "Twas the Night before Christmas", first published anonymously in 1823, and widely reprinted, both invented and popularized the tradition of hanging stockings on Christmas Eve. Moore did not take credit for writing the poem until 1837.

48. True. Compared to Christmas trees, Christmas stockings have barely changed since their introduction in the 1820s. Trees have changed in terms of how they are decorated, where the presents are placed, and what sorts of presents are with them.

49. B. Christmas trees are coniferous, also called evergreen trees. Douglas Fir and Scotch Pine are two of the most common trees grown for Christmas trees. Scotch Pine take about seven or eight years to grow to Christmas tree size in a plantation setting and Douglas Fir take about seven to ten years to grow to Christmas tree size in a plantation setting. Today most natural Christmas trees come from plantations rather than forests.

50. A. The concept of a Christmas tree was brought to the United States by immigrants from Germany. At first Christmas trees were only common in German-American communities. In the 1850s Christmas trees became popular nationwide thanks in part to the lobbying efforts of magazines such as Godey's. The editor of Godey's, Sarah J. Hale, was a champion of holidays and a social customs arbitrator. Christmas trees were popularized by magazine illustrations featuring Queen Victoria and Prince Albert of the United Kingdom gathered around a Christmas tree. (The illustrations were slightly modified to give the royal couple a more middle class appearance.) These illustrations did a lot to standardize what a Christmas tree should look like in terms of size and shape.

51. True. Martin Luther has been credited with the idea for Christmas trees. Likely Christmas trees existed before Luther's time. According to the legend, Luther was walking in the forest at night and saw the many stars in the sky and was inspired to bring a pine tree into his home and light it with candles.

52. A. Saint Boniface is another legendary originator of Christmas trees. According to legend, Saint Boniface stopped a pagan ritual by chopping down an oak tree that was

part of the ritual. An evergreen tree grew in the place of the oak tree and Saint Boniface suggested that people bring evergreen trees into their homes as a reminder of the Holy Trinity.

53. A. Some authorities argue that while bringing greenery into homes in the winter was a pre-Christian idea, actually bringing whole trees into homes did not develop until well into the Middle Ages and grew out of Christian Biblical plays. December 24 was a traditional day for the performance of a play about the Garden of Eden and so trees were hung with red balls which represented apples on the Tree of Knowledge of Good and Evil. These trees became Christmas trees.

54. B. Most historians conclude that Christmas trees are among the many pagan symbols that became Christianized and/or secularized. This relationship between pagan winter symbols and modern Christmas symbols will be discussed in further questions and answers throughout the book.

55. B. The original Christmas trees from the 1500s were unlighted and separate lights (candles) were used in homes for decorating. By the 1700s these had been combined with lighted trees as decorations. Unlit greenery and lit candles also remained as independent decorations.

56. A. In Germany, originally small trees (both real and artificial) were used, and gradually larger trees were used. Also originally each child had his or her own small tree. By the time Christmas trees spread to Britain and the United States, the trees were fairly close in size to the typical trees of today. As with many customs there were regional variations in how Christmas greenery and Christmas trees were displayed in the home, including variations in the type, the size of trees, and how they were displayed in the home.

57. C. Electric lights were first put on Christmas trees in the 1880s. Dual strand lights (the electricity travels on two wires instead of one so that one bulb burning out does not cause the whole strand to go dark) were invented and first used on Christmas trees in the 1920s.

58. A. In the 1500s, generally Christmas trees were only common in what is now Germany. Although people in many other countries throughout Europe decorated with greenery inside of the home, they did not use whole trees or decorations shaped like trees.

59. C. In the 1600s, Christmas trees were lit with candles for the first time. Previously candles had been used as a decoration but they had not been combined with Christmas trees.

60. D. In the 1850s, Christmas trees were rapidly gaining in popularity across the United States; previously their popularity had been largely confined to German-immigrant communities.

61. B. In the 1900s, Christmas trees were being lit with electric lights for the first time as the availability of electricity increased.

62. True. Mass production and the industrial revolution created great advances in worker productivity, meaning workers could make more goods at lower cost. These productivity advances led to economic gains and helped to raise the standard of living. These productivity gains ultimately led to a much larger middle class that was able to both produce and afford large quantities of Christmas presents. Prior to the industrial revolution, gift-giving was not a significant part of Christmas celebrations, even back into pre-Christian pagan times.

63. B. Christmas-themed store window displays became common in the 1870s. These eye-catching displays were meant to draw shoppers into the store to buy the perfect gift.

64. C. Christmas presents are wrapped to make them special. They are also traditionally wrapped to hide the fact that they were purchased at a store rather than being homemade.

65. A. The founder of Hallmark™, Joyce Hall, invented wrapping paper during World War I. The first wrapping paper was white with no design. The first wrapping paper with a printed design, had a holly pattern printed on it.

66. B. Tape for wrapping packages was invented in the 1930s. Previously wrapping paper had been secured with folds, and with ribbons or string.

67. A. Presents started small and got larger. Presents used to be hung on Christmas trees but in the 1890s heavy presents became common and presents began to be routinely placed below the tree. Early presents tended to be homemade. Early presents also tended to be novelty items rather than practical ones. The larger presents tended to be

more practical. The 1890s also marked the advertisers really getting into marketing Christmas gifts.

68. C. Generally prior to the 1890s, most Christmas presents were what today would be classified as stocking-stuffers. They tended to be gimmicky little devices of low quality with little practical value. The 1890s marked the decade when retailers everywhere got into the spirit of Christmas merchandizing and the value and quality of Christmas gifts increased.

69. B. Christmas trees in the 1880s were sometimes known as sugar trees because of all the candy presents that would be hanging on them. Gifts for adults prior to the 1890s tended to be minor trinkets. Gifts for children prior to the 1890s tended to be mostly candy and sweets.

70. B. The first electric toy train was sold by Lionel™ in 1904. Toy trains are a classic Christmas present.

CHRISTMAS FOODS

71. B. Nutmeg is the primary spice in eggnog.

72. A. Gingerbread houses originated in Germany. Nürnberg is noted for its fine gingerbread.

73. A. Ginger-flavored cookies and treats have been popular at Christmastime since the Middle Ages. There are many regional variations of ginger cookies. German *lebkuchen*, and Swedish *pepparkakor* are just two examples.

74. False. Plums are not usually an ingredient in plum pudding. The plum in plum pudding refers to the pudding being swollen. Plum is an old synonym for swollen. Plum puddings are served in spectacular fashion: often doused with hard liquor and set aflame before being brought to the table. Typically plum pudding includes raisins or currants. On rare occasions prunes (dried plums) are in plum pudding. Plum pudding is also sometimes called figgy pudding. It does not have figs in it either. The word fig used to be a synonym for raisin.

75. B. Buttered toast is a traditional ingredient in wassail. It is the origin of the meaning of the word "toast" referring to drinking a beverage for someone's good health. Wassail usually refers to a hot-spiced drink consumed at Christmastime. Many modern wassail recipes include apples and ale. Very few include toast. Wassailing includes going around the neighborhood with wassail cups or bowls which would be filled at each house and each host would be "toasted". Wassailing traditionally concludes with a ritual in an apple orchard that presumably was once connected to pagan agricultural customs.

76. A. *Buche de Noël* is a sponge cake shaped like a Yule Log, including chocolate frosting that is expertly crafted to look like real tree bark.

77. B. Oysters are a traditional Christmas food in France (among many other foods, of course). 70% of the oysters consumed in France are eaten at Christmastime.

78. A. The main Christmas dinner, known as *Le Reveillon de Noël,* is traditionally eaten after midnight mass on Christmas Eve. In larger cities, many restaurants are open all night to serve this meal. *Reveillon* means awakening.

79. True. *Foie gras* (goose liver) is a traditional Christmas gift in France.

80. C. Also known as an Epiphany cake, *Galette des Rois* is a cake eaten on Epiphany (January 6). Epiphany is the celebration of the arrival of the Wise Men. The cake contains a prize and a paper crown. The person who gets the prize gets to wear the crown and be king or queen for the day. There are many different regional varieties of *Galette des Rois* in France. Some cakes are more like shortbread, while other cakes are fruit-flavored or have sweet-tasting filling inside them.

81. A. Eels are a traditional Christmas food in Italy. Eels are the traditional main course for Christmas Eve dinner.

82. True. Pasta is eaten as part of the Christmas dinner in Italy. On Christmas Eve, often a fast leads up to a special meal featuring pasta, eels, and fried vegetables.

83. B. Fruitcake called *panettone* is a traditional Christmastime dessert in Italy. There are several regional varieties including *panforte, pandolce,* and *struffoli.*

84. B. Initial-shaped pastries are called *letterbankets.* They are eaten as part of the Feast of Saint Nicholas in Holland.

85. C. Saffron is the primary spice in Swedish baked goods for Saint Lucia Day (December 13). Saint Lucia was from Sicily and was martyred in Rome in the 300s. She brought food to Christians hiding in caves. She put candles on her head to light her path as she carried food to the Christians. She is a popular saint in Norway and Sweden.

86. B. Ham is traditionally eaten on Christmas in Sweden. It is known as *jul skinka* or Christmas ham. The custom of eating pork at Yule is an ancient one.

87. B. *Stollen* is a fruit bread shaped like a crib that is eaten in Germany.

88. B. Poppy-seed cake is the traditional dessert at a Polish *Wigilia. Wigilia* means vigil and it is a meal eaten in the evening of Christmas Eve while waiting for the arrival of Jesus. Often at the *Wigilia,* an extra place is set for Jesus.

89. B. *Babka* is a coffee cake that is a traditional Russian Christmastime food.

90. A. *Tourtière* is a pork pie that is eaten in Canada. It is traditionally eaten after a late-night Christmas Eve service. It is popular among the French-speakers of Quebec.

91. B. *Flan* is eaten in the Philippines. *Flan* is a type of cake.

92. B. *Buñuelo* is a Mexican pastry that is eaten at Christmastime. It is flat and round and covered with cinnamon and sugar.

93. C. *Oplatek* is eaten in Poland. It is unleavened bread stamped with an image of the Nativity.

94. C. Rice pudding called *risgrynsgröt* is served in Sweden. It is traditional to say a rhyme before eating a first bite of it at Christmas.

CHRISTMAS AROUND THE WORLD

95. True. Although Canada has a strong British and French heritage, it also has a lot in common with its neighbor to the south. Santa Claus is a common part of Christmas celebrations in Canada.

96. C. Vancouver, British Columbia, features a Christmas flotilla each year. The flotilla occurs two weeks before Christmas. On the ships are children's choirs singing Christmas carols and creating a wonderful sound across the harbor.

97. A. *Belsnicklers* are masked, costumed, rowdy, mischief-makers. They go around the neighborhood making noise, causing trouble, and asking for treats during the 12 days of Christmas. When a *belsnickler* has been identified at a particular house he ceases to be rowdy. *Belsnicklers* may give candy to children at the houses that they visit. Rowdy behavior similar to that of the *belsnicklers* (such as going around making noise outside) used to be common in Britain and the United States at Christmas prior to the 1850s. The common complaint about such earlier Christmases was not materialism, rather it was about drunkenness and rowdy mischief.

98. A. Father Christmas brings presents to British children. Like *Père Noël* and Santa Claus, he is a comparative newcomer to the Christmas holiday. He also brings his gifts on Christmas Eve.

99. B. Father Christmas originated in Victorian times as a combination of the ancient Celtic Frost Kings, Norse myths about Odin, and Victorian Christmas revelry. Later in the Victorian era, he brought gifts and began to more closely resemble Santa Claus rather than a figure from a pagan winter festival.

100. A. Christmas crackers were invented by candy-maker Thomas Smith in 1846. Christmas crackers make a delightful pop when they are pulled apart, revealing a small prize. They have been a popular Christmas tradition in Britain since soon after they were invented.

101. C. Boxing Day, also known as Saint Stephen's Day, is December 26.

102. C. Traditionally on Boxing Day, churches would give money to the poor and workers would collect a bonus from their employer. It is traditional to give an extra tip to service workers on Boxing Day.

103. True. Originally the Boxing Day bonus was collected in a ceramic box with a slot for money. However there was no way to open the box except by breaking it. These boxes got the nickname of "piggy". From these boxes came the pig-shaped reusable banks known as piggy banks.

104. B. *Père Noël* brings presents to French children. *Père Noël* is a 20th century French version of Saint Nicholas. However, *Père Noël* brings gifts on Christmas Eve rather than the night of December 5 like Saint Nicholas. He usually places his gifts in shoes that have been left out for that purpose.

105. A. In many homes in France, the centerpiece of the Christmas decorations is likely to be the *crèche* (manger display). Accompanying the *crèche* are little clay figures called *santons*. *Santons* depict a wide range of people and can include modern figures as well as traditional ones.

106. B. Setting up miniature winter village displays with model homes and shops was popularized in Germany. The displays are known as *putz*. Some *putz* are very elaborate, filling whole rooms with entire villages in miniature. Such miniature displays are also popular in the United States (and other countries) but tend to be smaller and less elaborate.

107. B. Germany is most famous for month-long Christmas markets.

108. A. *Julenisse* is a Christmas elf. He brings presents in Norway. He has a flowing white beard and a red cap. If not placated with gifts of cookies or porridge he can be mischievous.

109. True. Many children in Italy receive presents on both December 25 and January 6. *Befana* is the legendary gift-bringer in many parts of Italy. Many Italian children also receive presents on December 25 from either the Baby Jesus or Father Christmas. Italy is not the only country with two days for presents. For example, in Austria children also receive gifts on both Saint Nicholas's Day and Christmas.

110. B. Gifts in Greece are exchanged on January 1. January 1 is Saint Basil's Day. Saint Basil was one of the four founders of the Greek Orthodox Church. Scotland is another country where gifts are exchanged on January 1.

111. C. The Christmas season in Sweden ends on January 13. January 13 is Saint Knut's Day. Knut was a medieval king of Sweden who was known for his kindness and generosity.

112. C. Given the warmer outdoor weather in the southern hemisphere, outdoor sporting events are common, including horse racing in Chile and bullfighting in Peru. Christmas is also an important religious holiday in South America.

113. C. Children in Chile receive presents on January 6.

114. B. Children in Colombia receive presents on December 25. The presents are said to have been brought by the Baby Jesus on Christmas Eve. This is different than most countries in South America, where children receive presents from the Three Kings on January 6.

115. C. Children from Guatemala find gifts in their shoes on the morning of January 6. This is Epiphany and is also known as *el Dia de los Reyes*, (Day of the Kings). Part of the Christmas celebrations in Guatemala includes a midnight mass on Christmas Eve is known as *Misa de Gallo* (Mass of the Rooster). Roosters are believed to have crowed at midnight when Jesus was born. After the mass, fireworks are set off and bells are rung.

116. B. *Feliz Navidad* (Happy Christmas) is the Christmas greeting in Guatemala.

117. B. Poinsettias are flowering plants that originated in Mexico. They are named for Joel Robert Poinsett who served as U.S. Ambassador to Mexico from 1825 to 1829. They are also known as *Flor de Noche Buena* (Flower of the Holy Night). From their shape they are said to be symbols of the Bethlehem Star.

118. B. *Posadas* are nightly processions that take place from December 16 through the night of December 23. These processions involve going to a different house each night as the Holy Family seeking shelter. At each house a party is held. On December 24, the procession goes to church and the baby Jesus is added to the church Nativity display known as a *nacimiento*.

119. B. Part of the Christmas festivities in Oaxaca, Mexico include the Night of the Radishes. This local festival dates from the early 20th century and involves elaborate carving of radishes as part of a Christmas festival. The large radishes are carved with a wide range of designs, some that are from the Christmas story and others that are not.

120. C. Like in Guatemala, Mexican children receive presents on January 6 from the Three Kings.

121. C. The Christmas season ends in Mexico on February 2 with Candlemas (*Dia de la Candelario*). This worship service celebrates when Jesus was brought to the Temple.

122. B. Ethiopia celebrates *Timkat*, a holiday that celebrates the baptism of Christ. The three-day holiday begins on January 19. The Coptic Church in Ethiopia celebrates Christmas on January 7 (on the Gregorian Calendar). Feasting and sports are a large part of the Ethiopian Christmas celebration. Gift-giving is a very small part of Christmas in Ethiopia.

123. A. The Western and Eastern Churches are on different calendars and celebrate different events in the life of Jesus on Epiphany. Both Churches celebrate Epiphany on January 6. The Julian Calendar runs behind the Gregorian Calendar. January 6 on the Julian Calendar falls on January 19 on the Gregorian Calendar. The Western Churches celebrate the arrival of the Wise Men on January 6. The Eastern Churches celebrate the Baptism of Christ on January 6.

124. C. Christians in Egypt celebrate Christmas on January 7 according to the Gregorian Calendar. This date discrepancy is because they are among the Christians who follow the Julian Calendar, rather than the Gregorian Calendar. (According to the Julian Calendar, they are celebrating on December 25.) Christmas in Egypt is preceded by a 40 day fast from eating meat. This fast is known as *Kiahk*. Egyptian Christians attend a Christmas Eve service followed by the main Christmas dinner. At Christmas Day parties, children are given money called *El 'aidia*. This money is used to buy toys and candy.

125. A. A camel is said to bring Christmas presents to children in Lebanon.

126. B. In Lebanon, new seeds are planted in pots a few weeks before Christmas, and at Christmas, the seeds have begun to sprout. This makes for wonderful symbolism of new life in Christ.

127. B. Star lanterns (*parols*) are a featured Christmas decoration in the Philippines. The Philippines is the only Christian-majority nation in Asia.

128. B. Christmas services on December 25 in the Philippines feature Nativity plays called *Pastores*.

129. A. Christmas is celebrated in Japan like it is in the United States with many of the familiar decorations, and with Christmas trees and presents. However, there are relatively few Christians in Japan, so most Japanese only observe the secular customs of Christmas. Christmas is considered a time of fun and gifts.

130. C. The Christians in South Korea celebrate Christmas with early morning caroling that takes place around 2 am on Christmas morning. Christmas is mostly a religious observance in South Korea.

131. C. *Sheng Dan Lao Ren* is the Chinese name for Santa Claus. It translates as "Christmas Old Man". Santa is depicted in China as a man with a white beard and red silken robes. Many Chinese who are not Christian still participate in the secular parts of Christmas such as exchanging gifts and hanging stockings.

132. B. Summertime community candlelight caroling in city parks is part of the Australian Christmas. It has been a tradition in Australia since 1937. It was started by a radio announcer named Norman Banks.

133. C. Australian children leave lemonade out for Santa. December in Australia falls in the summertime rather than the winter. Santa appreciates the cool drink as he brings gifts to Australian children.

CHRISTMAS DECORATIONS AND SYMBOLS

134. A. Red and green are Christmas colors. It is thought that the red and green of holly is the source of these colors but that is not certain.

135. True. Many Christmas symbols and decorations include depictions of animals, objects, and characters from the Biblical story of Jesus's birth. Some examples: stars, angels, shepherds, sheep, Wise Men, Mary, Joseph, and the Baby Jesus. To this group of symbols and decorations are added many items that are not specifically mentioned in the Biblical account of the Nativity but fit into the story. For example: camels (for the Wise Men), a donkey (for Mary), a cradle, and a stable. Cookie-cutters and tree ornaments are often patterned after the examples listed in this answer.

136. True. Many Christmas symbols and decorations include depictions of objects that are part of celebrating Christmas. For example: bells, candles, candy canes, Santa Claus, reindeer, and Christmas trees. Like the symbols in the previous question, cookie-cutters and tree ornaments are often patterned after the examples listed in this answer. Many of these decorations that symbolize Christmas also have their own separate meaning. Some of these separate meanings are discussed in further questions in this section.

137. C. An Advent Wreath is generally a wreath with four candles in it. Each candle represents one of the four Sundays in Advent. Advent is about preparing for the coming of Christ.

138. C. Candy canes symbolize a shepherd's crook. Candy canes are a reminder that Jesus is the Good Shepherd. All other elements of the candy cane can be symbols of Jesus. For example, it is a hard candy, symbolizing Jesus as the Rock.

139. B. A crown of thorns is an Easter symbol. It is not a Christmas symbol. Angels and wreaths are common Christmas symbols.

140. A. Red glass ball ornaments symbolize apples. These have their origins in medieval plays. It became traditional to have a play about the Garden of Eden on December 24th. The red ornaments symbolize fruit on the Tree of Knowledge. The trees from these plays were known as Paradise Trees. As noted earlier, some historians conclude that Paradise Trees were the forerunners to Christmas trees.

141. A. Religious artwork about the Nativity has been around since at least the 380s. Movable decorations featuring Mary and Joseph waiting for the Nativity have been around since at least the 1200s. Saint Francis of Assisi is credited with inventing these decorations as a means to teach the story of Jesus's birth to less-educated commoners in Italy. These movable Nativity decorations go by different names in different countries: *crèche*, *presepio*, and *nacimiento* are just a few examples.

142. C. The original Yule logs were supposed to provide enough light for the 12 nights of Christmas. Originally Yule logs were part of a pagan winter celebration. These logs were massive tree trunks and capable of burning for a long time if the fire was carefully tended.

143. B. Light at Christmas symbolizes Christ as Light of the World. Often this light takes the form of a lighted candle, either at home or in church services.

144. B. Outdoor electric Christmas lights became popular and common in the 1950s.

145. B. Mistletoe symbolizes Christ the Healer. Mistletoe was an important plant to the Celtic druids.

146. C. Holly symbolizes strength. Holly was another plant with mystical symbolism for the Celts that was adapted as a Christmas symbol. Holly is one of the Christmas decorations mentioned in Charles Dickens's *A Christmas Carol*.

147. B. Of the choices given, the holly best represents Christ's suffering with the crown of thorns, represented by spiny holly leaves, and the red berries representing drops of blood. Holly symbolically ties Christmas to Easter.

148. A. Ivy symbolizes human weakness clinging to divine strength. Ivy was a symbol of the Roman god of wine, Bacchus. Taverns often used pictures of ivy on their exterior signs to tell illiterate customers what was sold there.

149. A. Bay (laurel) now symbolizes Christ's victory over sin and death. Previously laurel had been a symbol of the Roman emperor who was often insisted on being worshipped as a divine figure.

150. B. The cradle as a symbol of Christmas comes from Germany in the Middle Ages.

CHRISTMAS MUSIC

151. B. The earliest carols date from the 1200s and were in Italian. Sacred music prior to that time was only in Latin. Prior to the 19th century, carols were not generally sung in church.

152. C. "Silent Night". With lyrics like "all is calm", and "sleep in heavenly peace", "Silent Night" is among the most powerfully calm Christmas Carols.

153. C. One partridge, two turtles doves, three French hens, four calling birds, six geese, and seven swans make a total of 23 birds.

154. C. The carol "Jingle Bells" was first published in the 1850s. The song takes place at night. ("…O what fun it is to ride and sing a sleighing song tonight.")

155. A. Like the title suggests "Angels from the Realms of Glory" is about the angels. Verse 1: "Angels from the realms of glory, wing your flight o'er all the earth…"

156. B. "As with Gladness" is about the Magi. The Magi are also known as the Three Kings or the Three Wise Men. The carol opens "As with gladness men of old did the guiding star behold…".

157. C. "Go Tell It on the Mountain" is about the shepherds and their sharing the news of Jesus's birth everywhere. Verse 1: "While shepherds kept their watching…". See also Luke 2:17.

158. D. "The First Noel" is about all three: angels, shepherds and Magi. Verse 1: "The first Noel, the angel did say, was to certain poor shepherds in fields…" Verse 3: "And by the light of that same star, Three wise men came from country far…"

159. C. The third verse of "Silent Night" ends with "Jesus, Lord at thy birth".

160. True. "Thou Didst Leave Thy Throne refers to the Second Coming in the fifth verse. Verse 5: "When the heavens shall ring, and the angels sing, At Thy coming to victory, Let Thy voice call me home saying, "Yet, there is room, There is room at My side for thee." Refrain for fifth verse: "My heart shall rejoice, Lord Jesus! When Thou comest and callest for me."

161. B. All four verses of "There's a Song in the Air" end with "King". "There's a Song in the Air" was written by Dr. Josiah Holland, founder of <u>Scribner's</u> magazine.

162. A. "Born the King of angels" completes the phrase from the first verse of "O Come All Ye Faithful".

163. B. The angels in "It Came upon a Midnight Clear" have harps of gold. From verse 1: "…from angels bending near the earth to touch their harps of gold…".

164. B. The Child (Jesus) in "What Child Is This" is sleeping on Mary's lap. Verse 1: "What Child is this, who, laid to rest, on Mary's lap is sleeping…".

165. A. The angels in "Hark the Herald Angels Sing" sing "Glory to the newborn King" in the first line of the first verse of the song.

166. B. The cattle in "Away in a Manger" are lowing. Verse 2 begins: "The cattle are lowing…".

167. A. "Joy to the World" does not mention myrrh. "We Three Kings" refers to myrrh in verse 4. "What Child Is This" mentions myrrh in verse 3.

168. A. "Angels We Have Heard on High" urges hearers to "Come to Bethlehem and see Him whose birth the angels sing; come adore on bended knee, Christ the Lord, the newborn King."

169. B. "Jingle Bells" was first sung by a Boston Sunday School class around Thanksgiving-time in 1858.

170. A. "Santa Claus is Coming to Town" was written in 1934, during the Great Depression.

171. C. "Go Tell It on the Mountain" was first published in 1907. Many spirituals were sung and taught for years before being written down.

172. B. "Rise Up Shepherds and Follow" is a spiritual. Spirituals are from the African-American community and come from an oral tradition.

173. B. "Angels from the Realms of Glory" is based on Job 38:7. That Bible verse refers to angels. The song in question refers to angels and the other choices given do not deal with angels.

174. A. The carol "Good Christian Men Rejoice" is based on an earlier Latin hymn, "In Sweet Shouting".

175. B. "Away in a Manger" originally had two verses. The third verse was added later. Martin Luther is credited with writing "Away in a Manger." This may have just been a marketing ploy by the publisher as it is likely that the carol was written a century or two after Luther.

176. A. "I Heard the Bells on Christmas" was written by famous poet Henry Longfellow. He wrote the words in the midst of the American Civil War. The song has seven verses. Sometimes the verses with direct references to the war with lines like "cannon thundered in the South…" are omitted from hymnals. The verse "Then pealed the bells more loud and deep: God is not dead: nor doth He sleep; the wrong shall fail, the right prevail, with peace on earth, good-will to men" is a powerful testimony about the goodness of God that happens on God's time rather than on human time.

177. A. "O Come All Ye Faithful" is generally regarded as the second-most-widely-translated carol. "Silent Night" has been translated into more languages than any other carol. Both have been translated into over 100 languages.

178. A. "O Little Town of Bethlehem" was inspired by the songwriter's trip to Bethlehem in the 1860s.

179. C. "Joy to the World" is set to music from Handel's *Messiah*. The custom of standing for the "Hallelujah Chorus" comes from King George II who was so moved by the music and words when he heard it for the first time that he stood up in honor of Christ. His action began the tradition of standing for the "Hallelujah Chorus."

180. B. "O Come O Come Emmanuel" comes from a medieval liturgy.

181. C. "O Holy Night" was performed for the first time on Christmas Eve in 1847. The carol was first performed in France.

182. A. Composer Franz Grüber wrote the music to "Silent Night".

183. B. William Dix, author of the lyrics to "What Child Is This" and "As with Gladness" worked as an insurance salesman.

184. C. The first North American carol was sung in Huron. Jesuit missionaries in Canada translated the French carol "Jesus Is Born" into Huron in the 1640s, making it the earliest North American carol.

185. A. "Once in Royal David's City" was written by a woman named Cecil Frances Alexander, who was a pioneer in the concept of Sunday School. The song first appeared in a children's hymnal published in 1849.

186. A. "The First Noel" was generally sung outdoors at Yule Log ceremonies. Yule logs are another ancient custom that was Christianized and allowed to remain part of the Christmas celebration. Yule logs were most popular in France. They are much less common now.

187. A. Christina Rossetti wrote a poem called "A Christmas Carol" which was later adapted into the carol "In the Bleak Midwinter".

188. C. Old legends that are from the Middle Ages if not older, suggest that animals gain the power of speech at midnight on Christmas and that is the inspiration behind "The Friendly Beasts".

189. C. In addition to being based on Luke 2:13, "Hark the Herald Angels Sing" is based on 2 Corinthians 5:19 which, like the song, refers to the reconciliation between God and humankind. "Hark the Herald Angels Sing" was written by poet Charles Wesley in the 1700s. Charles had a famous brother named John Wesley. Although a life-long Anglican, John Wesley is considered to be the founder of the Methodist Church.

CHRISTMAS IN BOOKS AND MOVIES

190. True. *Little Women* includes a Christmas episode that shows Christmas giving as an expression of love. *Little Women* was written in 1868, around the time that Christmas became a very popular national holiday.

191. A. Edmund Gwenn's beard and weight were real, adding to the realism of his Oscar-winning portrayal of Santa in *Miracle on 34th Street* (1947).

192. B. In the Sherlock Holmes mystery, "The Adventure of the Blue Carbuncle" which takes place at Christmastime, a Christmas goose is involved in a case of mistaken identity. This short story is a classic Sherlock Holmes mystery and worth reading.

193. C. In "Papa Panov" the message of the story is to treat everyone like you would treat Jesus. It goes almost without saying that this story is definitely worth reading.

194. C. Four spirits appear in *A Christmas Carol*. The spirits are Jacob Marley, the Ghost of Christmas Past, the Ghost of Christmas Present, and the Ghost of Christmas Future.

195. B. The greedy miser in *A Christmas Carol* is named Ebenezer Scrooge.

196. B. The movie *Jingle All the Way* features Arnold Schwarzenegger as a dad attempting to make amends to his wife and son by purchasing a particular, hard-to-find toy as a Christmas present.

197. A. Ralphie is desperate for a BB gun in the movie *A Christmas Story*.

198. True. Julia Dreyfus (Elaine from "Seinfeld") portrays one of the neighbors in *Christmas Vacation*.

199. B. The award-winning young children's story *Polar Express* features a boy riding a train to the North Pole. The boy later meets Santa and is given a special bell.

200. A. The Grinch disguises his dog as a reindeer in the classic children's story *How the Grinch Stole Christmas*.

201. C. The man in the O. Henry short story "The Gift of the Magi" sells his watch.

202. C. Author Louisa May Alcott also wrote about Thanksgiving.

203. C. Writer Katherine Lee Bates contributed the ideas that (A) Santa gets hungry while delivering presents and should be left a snack and also (B) that Santa is married.

204. C. Charlie Brown buys a small real Christmas tree in the *A Charlie Brown Christmas*.

205. A. *It's a Wonderful Life* features two characters named Bert and Ernie. Contrary to rumor, Bert and Ernie from Sesame Street are not named after the characters from *It's a Wonderful Life*.

206. A. "Christmas Day in the Morning" is about the importance of saying "I love you". Choice B is on the right track but A is closer to the message expressed in the story -- be sure to tell a loved one that you love him or her.

207. A. Ramona's sister Beezus plays Mary in the Christmas pageant in *Ramona and Her Father*.

208. C. Each verse of the carol in *The Wind and the Willows* ends with a phrase very similar to "joy in the morning". (The phrase is not identical in each verse). The carol mentions both Mary and Joseph and the Nativity, but does not specifically mention Jesus.

209. A. The oxen are kneeling and the poem makes it clear that they are doing so in homage.

210. True. G.K. Chesterton wrote a poem about the Nativity called "A Christmas Carol".

211. C. The narrator in "Christmas at Sea" expresses regret that he is away from home at Christmas.

212. C. Laura is concerned in *Little House in the Big Woods* that Santa will not come unless she falls asleep. Santa will not come if she is awake, according to Laura.

213. C. In *Little House on the Prairie*, Laura receives two edible and two inedible items in her stocking. She receives a tin cup, a penny, peppermint candy, and a sugary treat.

214. B. The evil White Witch keeps Narnia in a perpetual state of winter and never Christmas until Aslan intervenes.

CHRISTMAS IN THE BIBLE

215. A. Caesar Augustus decreed a census. Quirinius was governor of Syria. See Luke 2:1-3.

216. A. Jesus was born in Bethlehem. See Matthew 2:1, Luke 2:4.

217. B. Jesus was born in the stable because there was no room at the inn. See Luke 2:7.

218. C. The stables mentioned in the Gospel of Saint Luke were likely in a small cave.

219. A. Jesus's birth was first announced to shepherds. See Luke 2:8-15.

220. C. The wise men saw a star in the East. See Matthew 2:1-12.

221. A. Yes, there are independent astronomical observances that could be the star mentioned in the Bible. Possibilities include a supernova, a planetary conjunction, and a comet, as well as combinations of these events.

222. C. The Wise Men brought gifts of gold, frankincense, and myrrh. See Matthew 2:11.

223. C. No exact number of Wise Men is given in the Bible. Three gifts are mentioned so traditionally it is assumed that there were three Wise Men.

224. A. The Gospel of Saint Matthew traces the genealogy of Christ back as far as Abraham. See Matthew 1:1-17.

225. C. The Gospel of Saint Luke traces Christ's genealogy is traced back to God and Jesus is proclaimed the Son of God. See Luke 3:23-37.

226. B. Elizabeth was the mother of John the Baptist. See Luke 1:13.

227. C. Zechariah was the father of John the Baptist. See Luke 1:13, 59-60.

228. A. The angel Gabriel appears to Mary. See Luke 1:26-38.

229. C. Another meaning for the word host is army. A heavenly host is an army of angels. See Luke 2:13.

230. C. Neither gospel mentions the donkey or the oxen that are often depicted in artwork involving the Nativity. However, Isaiah 1:3 mentions a donkey, oxen, and a manger. It is likely that this verse is the source of inspiration for including a donkey and oxen in the Nativity even though those animals are not mentioned in the gospel accounts.

231. B. The Gospel of Saint Luke has the story of Christ being presented at the Temple. See Luke 2:21-39.

232. B. Simeon blesses Jesus at the Temple. See Luke 2:28-35.

233. A. The Gospel of Saint Matthew has the story of the Magi. See Matthew 2:1-12.

234. A. The Gospel of Saint Matthew has the story of the flight to and later return from Egypt. See Matthew 2:13-19.

235. C. After Jesus's birth, all four gospels have the story of Jesus's baptism by John the Baptist. See Matthew 3:13-17, Mark 1:9-11, Luke 3:21-22, and John 1:26-34.

236. A. The book of Isaiah foretells the coming of Jesus and identifies him as the Prince of Peace. See Isaiah 9:6,7.

237. B. The book of Micah identifies that Jesus will be born in Bethlehem. See Micah 5:2,4.

238. A. Isaiah 9:6 also identifies Jesus as Wonderful Counselor.

239. C. The Gospel of Saint John identifies Jesus as the Light of the World. See John 1:6-14.

240. A. Christ means savior or anointed one in Greek. See Luke 2:11.

For further reading see *In the Fullness of Time*, cited in the Bibliography, for a theologian's research and conclusions about the surprising historical accuracy of the Bible, particularly in regards to the accounts of Christmas and Easter in the Bible.

CHRISTMAS CELEBRATION HISTORY

241. True. Easter was celebrated as a Christian holy day and holiday before Christmas became a Christian holy day and holiday. Within the Christian community, Easter became a widespread religious holiday in the 100s A.D. and Christmas became a widespread religious holiday in the 300s A.D.

242. C. *Samhain* is a Celtic festival that is celebrated on October 31, a date which clearly is not within a few weeks of the Winter Solstice. *Invictus Sol* was a Persian holiday that celebrated the unconquerable sun and was popular among the Romans. *Saturnalia* was a winter festival that was celebrated in late December. This particular question and answer is not an exhaustive list of pre-Christian winter festivals. The Norse also celebrated the Yule, as did the Celts. As part of Yule, Yule logs were burned in ceremonies to honor the return of the sun.

243. A. *Kalends* was the Ancient Roman New Year. Minor gifts were exchanged at this time. The custom of giving gifts on New Year's Day can be traced to *Kalends*.

244. True. There are wintertime gift-bringing legends associated with Odin. In disguise, Odin would spy on the Norse and might give bread to some good-hearted poor people.

245. D. None of the above best describes Christmas celebrations in 100 A.D. Christmas was not celebrated at that time.

246. B. Christmas in the year 400 A.D. was merely a religious observance. Early church leaders frowned on any behavior that was connected to any pagan practice. This strongly-worded quote from the theologian Tertullian is a good sound-bite summary of the attitude of the early church towards any pagan practice such as decorating with greenery during the wintertime:

> "Let them over whom the fires of hell are imminent, affix to their posts, laurels doomed presently to burn: to them the testimonies of darkness and the omens of their penalties are suitable. You are a light of the world, and a tree ever green. If you have renounced temples, make not your own gate a temple."

247. B. The Byzantine Empire was the first government to recognize Christmas as a legal holiday, doing so in 529 A.D. under the Emperor Justinian.

248. A. Christmas celebrations in England around 1400 A.D. included church services, but these services were overshadowed by feasting, pranks, and merry-making that took place around Christmastime. By the 1400s, the church leaders had long-since overruled the earlier precedent of not celebrating at Christmastime. In the 1400s observances that were not directly idolatry were ok as long as the practitioner's heart was turned toward Christianity. This meant that many unruly customs and folk traditions had been Christianized or secularized and were now a part of the extended Christmas celebration.

249. True. For most people Christmastime was a rare holiday from work during the year during the Middles Ages.

250. C. The Twelve Days of Christmas run from December 25 through January 6. Until the modern era of Christmas, the Twelve Days of Christmas were traditionally a time of much revelry. They trace their origins to pagan winter festivals.

251. B. The Lord of Misrule was elected to cause mischief during his term of office which ran during the 12 Days of Christmas. The Lord of Misrule is a custom that disappeared during the Puritan campaign against Christmas. Remnants of the rowdiness at Christmastime remained until the modern Christmas took shape and the secular focus of Christmas shifted from a rowdy party to family gift-giving. The Lord of Misrule comes from an Ancient Roman custom of masters and slaves trading places for a day.

252. A. Mummers are boisterous actors and street entertainers who are led by the Lord of Misrule. They would generally be rowdy and cause disruptions during the 12 Days of Christmas. They would also act out plays. These plays were about death and renewal. The mummers can be traced back to the Roman *Saturnalia* festival. The mummers and Lord of Misrule were abolished by the Puritans and the custom faded away.

253. C. The 12 Days of Christmas culminate on the Twelfth Night, which takes place on January 5. The 12 Days of Christmas is a time for partying, feasting, and merry-making. The Twelfth Night is the biggest party. The next day, January 6, Epiphany, is a holy day and marks the end of the 12 Days of Christmas. At the Twelfth Night party, a special cake is eaten and the person who gets the bean in his or her slice of cake becomes the king or queen of the party. The drawback is that person must host the Twelfth Night party next year. The 12 Days of Christmas is another pre-Christian custom that became part of the secular Christmas celebration.

254. B. In the mid-1600s, in areas with Puritan influence (primarily England and the United States), Christmas celebrations had been greatly curtailed or even banned. Christmas was a day of work, not a day of celebration and leisure. These Christmas bans were in reaction to the perceived excesses of earlier celebrations. In the parts of the world where Catholic and Orthodox churches were dominant, Christmas was still celebrated as a blend of pious church attendance and local traditions.

255. B. The modern American Christmas really began to take shape in the 1860s.

256. A. Franklin Pierce (president 1853-1857) was the first president to have a Christmas tree. It was not an official government tree. It was only displayed in the private presidential residence. The first national Christmas tree in the U.S. was displayed in Washington D.C. in 1923.

257. A. The Civil War and Reconstruction helped spread and strengthen the importance of Christmas as a national holiday. A Christmas celebration offered a family-centered holiday in a time of turmoil and also helped reunify the country after the Civil War.

258. C. In 1870, in the same law, Christmas and Thanksgiving were among the five holidays established as federal holidays. Interestingly, the date of Thanksgiving was not set by that initial legislation. It was left to the president to continue a tradition of declaring a Day of Thanksgiving. Usually this day was the fourth Thursday in November. In 1939 and 1940, President Franklin Roosevelt declared the third Thursday to be Thanksgiving. He did so to try and boost Christmas sales. The change from tradition was unpopular and in December of 1941, Congress passed a law that President Roosevelt signed which established Thanksgiving as the fourth Thursday in November. In practice, Thanksgiving and Christmas have both been celebrated nationwide in America since the 1860s.

259. True. The early 1900s represented the high water mark for public feasts for the poor on Christmas Day. Perhaps inspired by Charles Dickens, in the late 19th century these feasts were common across the country; many of these feasts served thousands of poor people. At the largest of these feasts, the Salvation Army served over 25,000 people at Madison Square Garden in New York City in 1903. World War I and criticism that the feasts were inefficient at helping the poor get out of poverty led to a decline in these public feasts. Today with much less fanfare and publicity, many charity organizations and churches still provide meals for the poor at Christmas and these meals are greatly appreciated.

260. B. Since the 1920s, the basic shape of Christmas observances in America has remained unchanged. Considering all of the other things that have changed so much since then, it is remarkable how stable Christmas celebrations have been.

261. B. Pope Gregory I was one of the church leaders who recognized that an overly strict interpretation of what is idolatry and what is not would turn people away from Christianity rather than towards it. Under his leadership, many pagan practices and beliefs were outlawed. However those practices that did not come into conflict with Christianity were allowed to remain even though the practice originated as a part of pagan worship.

"The idol temples of that race should by no means be destroyed, but only the idols in them. Take holy water and sprinkle it in these shrines, build altars and place relics in them. For if the shrines are well built, it is essential they should be changed from the worship of the devils to the service of the true God. When this people see that their shrines are not destroyed they will be able to banish error from their hearts and be more ready to come to the places they are familiar with, but now recognizing and worshipping the true God."
-Pope Gregory I in a statement written circa 500 A.D.

262. C. By 2000 A.D., the dominant focus of Christmas as observed by the people of the United States as a whole had turned to gift-giving. This answer is not meant to diminish the religious side of Christmas. Church attendance on December 24th and/or December 25th is very high. For many people Christmas is both a secular and a sacred holiday. As this book shows, since the early days of Christmas, there has always been this tension between sacred and secular observances of the holiday. (If you have enjoyed this book and would like to learn more about Christian holidays that have a secular side to them, see my trivia books about Easter and Halloween).

CONCLUSION

Christmas is a wonderful holiday! From the divine messages it carries with news of Jesus's birth, to the human joy found in celebration, Christmas is a great source of happiness. I hope that these trivia questions help you to find happiness in Christmas; whether that happiness comes from a Christian message, the joy of spending time with family, great food, parties, the fun of family and cultural traditions, charity for others, a tree laden with ornaments, the joy of exchanging gifts, or all of the above! I hope this book helps you to embrace both the sacred and the secular traditions of Christmas with a smile on your face and joy in your heart!

Merry Christmas!

SCORING

<u>Percentage Correct</u>

100%: You would be ready to take his place should anything happen to Santa!

90-99%: Clearly with your knowledge you could write an encyclopedia about Christmas

80-89%: If there is a job vacancy in Santa's workshop – you should consider applying

70-79%: Frosty the Snowman is proud of you!

60-69%: Santa's reindeer are pleased with your score

50-59%: A fine showing. Perhaps you are also a scholar of Christmas

40-49%: Not too bad, the Whos in Whoville will sing your praises

30-39%: Rudolph says you can do better!

20-29%: Did the Grinch steal some of your correct answers?

10-19%: Every reindeer has his day and maybe today is not your day

1-9%: Perhaps you forgot to have some milk and (Christmas) cookies before taking this test?

0%: Oh my! Better check your score again

Regardless of how many you got correct, I hope these questions were fun and prompt you to learn more about Christmas!

Have a Merry Christmas!

BIBLIOGRAPHY

Bevilacqua, Michelle. *The Everything Christmas Book.* Holbrook, MA : Adams Media Corp, 1996.

Bordon, David and Winters, Tim. *Everything Christmas.* Colorado Springs, CO. : Waterbrook Press, 2010.

Bradley, Ian. *The Penguin Book of Carols.* London : Penguin, 1999.

Brown, Peter. *Through the Eye of a Needle : Wealth, the Fall of Rome, and the Making of Christianity in the West, 350-550 AD.* Princeton : Princeton University Press, 2012.

Carus, Louise. *The Real St. Nicholas : Tales of Generosity and Hope from Around the World.* Wheaton, IL : Quest Books, 2002.

Collins, Ace. *Stories Behind the Great Traditions of Christmas.* Grand Rapid, MI : Zondervan, 2003.

Ebon, Martin. *Saint Nicholas : Life and Legend.* New York : Harper, 1975.

Emurian, Ernest K. *Stories of Christmas Carols.* Grand Rapids, MI : Baker Books, 1996.

Forbes, Bruce D. *Christmas : A Candid History.* Los Angeles : University of California Press, 2007.

Fox, Dan. *A Treasury of Christmas Songs : Twenty-five Favorites to Sing and Play.* New York : Metropolitan Museum of Art : Henry Holt and Co., 2004.

Gibbons, Gail. *Santa Who?.* New York : Morrow Junior Books, 1999.

Ideals Publications. *Ideals Christmas,* Nashville, TN : Ideals Publications, 2010.

Ingalls, Ann. *Christmas Traditions around the World.* Mankato, MN : The Child's World, 2013.

Jeffers, H. Paul. *Legends of Santa Claus.* Minneapolis, MN : Lerner Publications, 2000.

Johnson, Paul. *A History of Christianity.* New York : Atheneum, 1976.

Jones, E. Willis. *The Santa Claus Book.* New York : Walker and Company, 1976.

Kennedy, Caroline. *A Family Christmas.* New York : Hyperion, 2007.

King, Constance. *Christmas : Antiques Decorations and Traditions.* Woodbridge, Suffolk, U.K. : Antique Collectors Club Ltd., 1999.

Kelley, Emily. *Christmas around the World.* Minneapolis, MN : Carolrhoda Books, Inc., 2004.

Kostyal, K.M. *Christmas in Williamsburg.* Washington D.C. : National Geographic Society, 2011.

Krythe, Maymie R. *All about Christmas.* New York : Harper Collins Juvenile Books, 1954.

Lankford, Mary D. *Christmas Around the World.* New York : Morrow Junior Books, 1995.

Marling, Karal Ann. *Merry Christmas! : Celebrating America's Greatest Holiday.* Cambridge, MA : Harvard University Press, 2000.

Matthews, John. *The Winter Solstice : The Sacred Traditions of Christmas.* Wheaton, IL : Quest Books, 1998.

Maier, Paul L. *In the Fullness of Time : A Historian Looks at Christmas, Easter, and the Early Church.* Grand Rapids, MI : Kregel Publications, 1997.

Miles, Clement A. *Christmas Customs and Traditions : Their History and Significance.* New York : Dover Publications, Inc., 1976.

Muir, Frank. *Christmas Customs & Traditions.* New York : Taplinger Pub. Co., 1977.

Nissenbaum, Stephen. *The Battle for Christmas : A Social and Cultural History of Christmas that Shows How It Was Transformed from an Unruly Carnival Season into the Quintessential American Family Holiday.* New York : Alfred A. Knopf, 1996.

Osbeck, Kenneth. *Joy to the World!.* Grand Rapids, MI : Kregel Publications, 1999.

Rau, Dana Meachen. *Christmas.* New York : Children's Press, 2000.

Restad, Penne L. *Christmas in America : A History.* New York : Oxford University Press, 1995.

Ridley, Jacqueline. *Christmas Around the World: A Celebration.* New Orchard Editions, 1985.

Rockwell, Mary. *Norman Rockwell's Christmas Book.* New York : Abrams, 1977.

Standiford, Les. *The Man Who Invented Christmas.* New York : Crown Publishers, 2008.

Steves, Rick and Griffith, Valerie. *Rick Steves' European Christmas.* Berkeley, CA : Avalon Travel, 2013.

Tucker, Cathy C. *Christmas Worldwide : A Guide to Customs and Traditions.* Philadelphia : Xlibris, 2000.

U.S. Committee for UNICEF. *Joy through the World.* New York : A. D. Bradgon Publishers; distributed by Dodd, Mead, 1985.

Walsh, Joseph. *Were They Wise Men or Kings? : the book of Christmas questions.* Louisville, KY : Westminster John Knox Press, 2001.

Whelchel, Lisa. *The ADVENTure of Christmas.* Sisters, OR : Multnomah Publishers, Inc., 2004.

Weiser, Franz Xaver. *Christmas Book.* New York : Harcourt, 1952.

Fiction:

Alcott, Louisa May. *Little Women.* New York : Scholastic Inc., 2000.

Baum, L. Frank. *The Life and Adventures of Santa Claus.* Ann Arbor, MI : Lowe & B. Hould, n.d. (Reprint of a book originally published in 1902).

Dickens, Charles. "A Christmas Carol" in *A Christmas Carol and Other Stories.* New York : Modern Library, 1995.

Doyle, Sir Arthur Conan. "The Adventure of the Blue Carbuncle" in *The Complete Sherlock Holmes Vol. 1.* New York : Barnes & Noble, 2003.

Foreman, Michael. *Michael Foreman's Christmas Treasury*. London : Pavilion Books Ltd., 1999.

Lewis, C.S. *The Lion, the Witch, and the Wardrobe*. New York : Harper Collins, 1994.

Nettell, Stephanie. *A Christmas Treasury*. New York : Penguin U.S.A., 1996.

Scarry, Richard. *Richard Scarry's Best Christmas Book Ever*. New York : Sterling, 1981.

Seuss, Dr. *How the Grinch Stole Christmas*. New York : Random House, 1957.

Tolstoy, Leo. *"Papa Panov's Special Christmas"*. Cedar Fort, Inc, 2011.

Van Allsburg, Chris. *The Polar Express*. Boston : Houghton Mifflin Company, 1985.

Movies and Television:

A Charlie Brown Christmas. Directed by Bill Melendez. 1965. Warner Home Video 2008, DVD.

A Christmas Carol. (Charles Dickens's classic story in movie form is also sometimes titled *Scrooge*) Many different movie versions of this story are available. I recommend trying at least 2). Consider the 1984 version with George C. Scott as Scrooge, or the Muppet's version with Michael Caine as Scrooge. See *Scrooge* below.

A Christmas Carol. Directed by Hugh Harman and Edwin Marin. 1938. Warner Home Video 2005, DVD. (Reginald Owen as Scrooge)

A Christmas Carol. Directed by Clive Donner. 1984. 20th Century Fox 1999, DVD. (George C. Scott as Scrooge)

A Christmas Carol. Directed by David Jones. Turner Home Entertainment 2000, DVD. (Patrick Stewart as Scrooge)

The Muppet Christmas Carol. Directed by Brian Henson. 1992. Walt Disney Home Entertainment 2012, DVD. (Michael Caine as Scrooge)

A Christmas Story. Directed by Bob Clark. 1983. Warner Home Video 1997, DVD.

Christmas Vacation. Directed by Jeremiah Chechik. 1989. Warner Home Video, 2008, DVD.

Home Alone. Directed by John Hughes. Twentieth Century Fox 1990. Fox Video 2006, DVD.

How the Grinch Stole Christmas!. Directed by Chuck Jones and Ben Washam. 1966. Warner Home Video 2009, DVD.

It's a Wonderful Life. Directed by Frank Capra. Liberty Films 1946. Republic Entertainment : Distributed by Artisan Entertainment, 1998, DVD.

Jingle All the Way. Directed by Brian Levant. 1996. 20th Century Fox 2007, DVD.

Miracle on 34th Street. Directed by George Seaton. 1947. 20th Century Fox Home Entertainment 2006, DVD.

Scrooge. Directed by Brian Desmond Hurst. 1951. VCI Entertainment 2011, DVD. (Alastair Sim as Scrooge)

Scrooge. Directed by Ronald Neame. 1970. Paramount 2003, DVD. (Albert Finney as Scrooge)

White Christmas. Directed by Michael Curtiz. 1954. Paramount 2009, DVD.

Websites:

http://www.biblegateway.org (This website has freely available many different translations of the Bible)

http://www.americancatholic.org (This website has many resources about the saints)

http://www.imdb.com (This website is a wealth of information about the cast and crew of movies.)

http://www.noradsanta.org (The website is active during December)

http://www.realchristmastrees.org/dnn/Education/TreeVarieties.aspx (Lots of information about commercially-grown Christmas trees)

http://www.stnicholascenter.org/pages/home/ (All about Saint Nicholas; an easy introductory resource compared to tracking down the Saint Nicholas-related books listed in the bibliography. Although, the books go into greater detail)

http://postalmuseum.si.edu/exhibits/current/customers-and-communities/serving-the-cities/overcoming-congestion/mail-by-motor.html (more about the postal crisis of 1913)

http://www.senate.gov/reference/resources/pdf/Federal_Holidays.pdf (Link to a PDF that gives a brief history of federal holidays)

ABOUT THE AUTHOR

The author is a lawyer who lives with his family near St. Paul, Minnesota. He has a B.A. in History/Political Science from the University of Jamestown, Jamestown, North Dakota and a J.D. from Hamline University School of Law, St. Paul, Minnesota. He has written more than half a dozen trivia books; including books about Easter, Halloween, Thanksgiving, U.S. presidents, and British monarchs.

47812338R00053

Made in the USA
Lexington, KY
14 December 2015